LOVE
BEADS
from
ELVIS

The Diary of Kathy Tatum

Kathy Tatum
with Mark Baker

Love Beads from Elvis
Copyright © 2015 by Kathy Tatum and Mark Baker
All rights reserved

Cover Design: Elizabeth E. Little
Interior Formatting: The Author's Mentor,
                www.LittleRoniPublishers.com

ISBN-13: 978-0692414040
ISBN-10: 0692414045
Also available in eBook

Fawnella/DeVille Media Partners
Collierville, TN

PUBLISHED IN THE UNITED STATES OF AMERICA

This book was written

to give my five children and five grandchildren a glimpse into a wonderful, exciting time of my life. Thanks to them for so much love and support throughout this adventure.

Thanks is not enough to say to my wonderful Momma and Daddy for a wonderful lifetime of amazing memories.

~Kathy

To Pauletta Seago!

Kathy Tatum

Mark Baker

Table of Contents

Preface

❧❧❧❧❧

I WASN'T LOOKING FOR IT...BUT I FOUND it just the same. It was near the back of my closet shelf, neatly sealed in a plastic bag along with some old pictures and notes. Seeing it again instantly brought back memories of times gone by and of a young girl's life I sometimes have trouble remembering. I removed it carefully from the bag and held it in my hands as I had so many times as a young girl. The hands which hold it now are ever so much older than fifteen. The red leather covering is well worn, and the locking clasp that once kept my secrets safe from the world is missing. There is duct tape on the binding, and the page edges have yellowed over time, but it is, after all, almost fifty years old.

I sat on the edge of my bed and debated with myself if I should just put it back in the bag. I knew who was written about in these pages and of the feelings and emotions it would once again stir. I thought about my children and my

1

grandchildren—it wasn't an easy decision to make. I suppose in the end, it was because of them I chose to share what is inside my diary with you. It is not my intention to tarnish the memories of those that are still with us. Rather, it is to share a lifetime of memories with my children and grandchildren; it is my legacy I leave to them.

I carefully open the diary's fragile cover, and on the first page it proclaims in the script of a fifteen year old girl,

FIVE YEAR DIARY
Property of: Kathy Tatum, Lynn

As I carefully turn the first page, an old Polaroid photo slips out. It is well worn, but the two in the picture are still recognizable. I remember quite vividly the night it was taken, and of how it had felt to be held in his strong arms. He was beautiful then—his skin tanned to a golden brown, and his jet black hair neatly combed straight back. I was surprised the first time I ran my fingers through it and found it to be as soft as silk, and not at all greasy. I can remember the way it felt when he gently kissed the back of my neck and sang softly into my ear. The feeling was like electricity through my body when he would tenderly kiss my fingertips. His lips were like the wings of a butterfly as he softly brushed my eyelashes. He would whisper his pet name for me, "Laughing Eyes," and I would all but melt in his arms. In the photo he still wears the love bead necklace that he would later place around my neck, sealed with a kiss. But this is not where the story begins. I suppose it could start *...Once upon a time...* isn't that how most children's fairy tales begin? Except, I was never a beautiful princess, at least I never thought so. I didn't live in a magical kingdom with a whimsical name, but rather in a mid-south city named Memphis. There was no shining castle atop a mountain bathed in a golden glow, but there was a storied mansion of white, known simply as Graceland. Contained within the pages of this true life fairy tale, there is no mention of a handsome prince. Instead, there was an extraordinary King...

4

The Diary of Kathy Tatum

1

～～～～～

AT THE TOP OF THE FIRST PAGE, IN BOLD print, is **January 1.** Underneath that, on the left side of the page, is 19__, left blank for the entry of a year. There are five narrow lines beneath, and below that is another 19__. Contained within that diminutive space, with each turn of the page, a small slice of my life would progress from one day to the next. At year's end it would return to the beginning and start anew. The handwriting is quite small. In some places it is hard for these tired eyes to read, but I suppose it was pretty good penmanship for my age. When I had a particularly exciting day, I would write extra details on slips of paper, sometimes on nothing but the flap of an old envelope. I used a different colored pen for each year, black, blue, etc., and it makes a pretty clear dividing line between the five years on each page. For some reason in 1970, I wrote entirely in red ink. In hindsight, it was probably not the best choice of colors, for it is the hardest of all to read. The first entry into the diary, in what was at the time a simple Christmas stocking stuffer, is dated…

December 29, 1967

… I turned down my first real date I was ever asked out on. George, Bob Wiley's cousin, is going skating with another couple. I didn't like him much anyway. He lived in Arkansas…

For me; reading that first entry felt as if I was prying into someone else's private thoughts. I guess in a way I was. This was a young girl who had lived a long time ago, in a much simpler time. Her life lay stretched out before her, and her heart was filled with hopes and dreams. In a strange way I envied her, but at the same time, I had no desire to relive that uncomfortable age. That most awkward period in a young girl's life, caught between a teen and a woman, was very confusing and emotional for me. It is inside the framework of that age, within the small diary spaces on the pages, she poured out her heart before going to bed. While she had no comprehension of what the next day would bring, in hindsight, I could still see the footprints in the sand of where she had already been. I closed my eyes and remembered…

My home…the home I had spent my entire life in until the day I married is still there. I drove by it the other day and just parked nearby and looked at it. It looks much the same as I remembered; it instantly flooded my heart with memories. In what was once surrounded by fields and flowers, the home now stands in an industrial park. One of the companies at the site is now using it for an office. The long gravel drive where my sisters and I used to ride our bikes is now a large paved parking lot for employees. The plum tree which once held our tree house has long ago succumbed to the ravages of weather and age. I guess it really wasn't much of a tree house after all, but actually just a couple of boards laid across some branches. Gone now, but not forgotten, as is the fate of all wondrous memories. Yet, as if in defiance of the progression of time, the house my daddy built by hand still stands.

Seeing the house once again gave me pause to reflect. There is much about my life that is not contained within these yellowed pages. My childhood memories, many as vivid as the day they happened, could not possibly fit within these small spaces. So many memories...

My daddy built the house I shared with my two sisters a couple of years before I was born. Terry was four years older than me, and Karen was five years younger. Daddy and mother had met on a blind date, and their love only grew over time. Daddy doted on mother for sixty-six years, until he died on this very day in June last year. Daddy's love for us was without limits, and he would have chopped off his own hand without question, if only I asked him to. Perhaps in some way, he is one of the reasons for baring what is written on the small spaces in this diary. His love for me would not have wavered in the least, even after learning what was kept hidden from him…so many years ago.

Before daddy retired, he worked for forty-two years making tires at the old Firestone plant in North Memphis. He worked in the tire mold division. I can remember his pride when the company celebrated its 100 millionth tire in Memphis. When he wasn't working a full day in the factory, he was doing everything else around our home, or helping friends. He would come home from work and immediately begin on something else, only quitting when it became too dark. Daddy was a deeply religious man and spent much of his free time involved with our church. There wasn't anything he couldn't do, but in the end he lost his battle with cancer at the age of 94. He was a most amazing man, and I still miss him so very much.

It was with a smile I read the next diary entry…

January 30, 1967

…I've had this feeling since I was in the 8th grade that when I got grown I would marry Ronnie Reaves. I was just writing this down where I would have proof in case I did marry him…

Although I would be married some five years after that entry, it would not be to Ronnie. I have no idea whatever happened to him, or for that matter, whatever made me want to marry him in the first place. I guess like most girls at the awkward age of 14, I just couldn't wait to be grown. Perhaps that is why as a child, I was always so fond of playing house. Even today, those are some of my fondest early memories.

I remember when I was about five years old my daddy gave me two rooms in the barn to use as my playhouse. I stacked bales of hay together to use as my couch and chairs, and I used bushel baskets turned upside down for my end tables. Daddy brought me an old water fountain from the church when they renovated it, and I propped it in the corner and used it for my sink. Mother gave me some old curtains and sheets to cover everything with, and it was just as nice as it could be. I would go into the pasture every morning and pick a large bundle of bitter weeds. Their white tops made perfect bouquets for my tables, and I fixed them in old vases mother had given to me.

The barn had a dirt floor, and I used daddy's broom to constantly sweep it. He would often smile and tell me, "Hon… you're about to drive me crazy just sweeping the dirt." I always knew it was only an old barn floor, but in my mind, these two rooms really were a house. Polk salad grew outside the barn door, and I thought it was the perfect place for my patio. Daddy found me some old bricks, and I laid them on the ground outside the door and made a patio of my very own. I wanted my house to be perfect. I suppose I was that way because of daddy; it's a side of my personality I would never outgrow.

When I was in the fourth grade, daddy built

me my own wooden playhouse. It was pretty big, about the size of a small shed, and had real shingles on the roof. Daddy got some old windows from the remodeled church and set them in the walls. He worked on it most every night--it was to be my Christmas present that year. I remember the old boards daddy used for the floor, and about how I wished I could have linoleum. He told me how sorry he was that I couldn't have it, and I would just have to make do with the rough wood floors. On Christmas morning, I went to the playhouse and found the most beautiful linoleum floor waiting for me. Daddy must have worked half the night to get it finished in time. As I said before, he was an amazing man and father.

Along with the shiny new floor, I found a completely furnished kitchen. It was made of pink pasteboard and consisted of a refrigerator, stove, and sink. Mother gave me some old curtains, which I used to cover my real windows. For me and my dolls, my playhouse became a special and magical place. For the next two years I practically lived in that playhouse. I ate my breakfast and lunch in that house almost every day, eating only dinner at the family table. All that changed following the Christmas when I was in the sixth grade. After our school break, I was crushed to learn that no other girl in the sixth grade received a doll for Christmas. For me, it was a painful lesson of the heart about growing up.

The world I had created within the walls of my playhouse ended just like that for me. If all my school friends were too grown up for dolls, then I guess I had to be too. I quit playing in the house after that, and there was never another doll under our tree for me again. I haven't really thought much about it until just now, but I guess it was the last real Christmas of my childhood. I wish now I had not been so easily influenced by others. I guess that is one of the hardest things about growing up and hope it is something my own grandchildren will be able to avoid.

The following Christmas, instead of a doll, daddy gave me my first real watch. It had diamond chips on each side of the watch face and a band made of brown leather. It was the first adult Christmas gift I had ever received, and oh how proud I was to wear it. I still have the watch today, for it is as special to me now as it was then. It rests safely in a velvet-lined box, next to the love beads Elvis once placed around my neck. They are both gifts which have deep feelings attached to them, for they are both from the men who will always have special places in my heart. I think I shall treasure them both forever.

When I was growing up, I didn't have a lot of friends because we lived so far out in the country. I went to Capleville Elementary School until the seventh grade. There probably weren't a hundred kids in the whole school. Most of them lived in subdivisions close to the school, so it was easy for them to hang around together. My older sister, Terry, had about three or four boys her age that lived in our neighborhood, and she hung around with them a lot. They would come over sometimes and we would play baseball in our yard. Even though they were older than me, I liked it when they would include me in their games. I guess being so much younger than them, I inevitably would get on their nerves.

Sometimes Terry would ask me to go into the house and ask mama something. It was always something silly, and I knew they were just trying to ditch me. She would tell me they wouldn't, but I didn't believe her. Still I would do it anyway, only to find out later they would all be gone somewhere without me. It would make me so mad when she would do that to me, but I spent so much time alone I was used to it and could always find something to do. Besides, it seemed like I always had a pet of some kind or another growing up, so I was never truly alone.

When I was about seven, I begged mother and daddy for a pet monkey. I wrote them a two or three page letter telling them why I needed a monkey, and please let me have a monkey. I never thought they would get me one, but one day daddy brought a squirrel monkey home from work. Someone he worked with had it and couldn't seem to do anything with it. He said it was wild as a goat and would bite anyone that tried to handle it, but my daddy brought it home anyway. He built a large cage for it, about four foot tall, and I named him Chico. I kept that cage spotless, and just like the man had told daddy, he really did try to bite everybody.

I had thick leather gloves to put on whenever I handled him, and after about a year he got used to me. He still tried to bite everyone else, but at least I no longer had to wear the gloves around him. I kept him on a small leash when he was out of his cage, and he would just sit on my shoulder everywhere I went. Sometimes he would escape from his cage and climb all over mama's curtains. I can still remember how mad she used to get. She would holler for me to come get him, and Chico always seemed to think it was a game when I chased him from window to window. He was so fast; it was almost impossible to catch him.

Most of the time whenever he got out, he would head straight for the sugar bowl on the kitchen table and poke his whole head down in it. I know he always made mother so upset, and I'm sure it didn't bother her too terribly when we finally gave him away. We never could seem to find anyone who would keep him when we went on vacations, so I gave him to a pet store in town. I cried when I left him, but I knew it was his best chance to find a good home.

After a while daddy got us a Shetland pony. It's funny how time can fade some memories, while leaving others untouched, but for the life of me I can't recall what we named him. I'm not even sure we named him at all, because we didn't have him very long. I do remember how pretty he was, and how much we loved riding him in the yard. Then one Sunday afternoon, he bucked off a little girl from the church, and daddy decided right then to give him away. He traded him to a man at work for an old swayback mare. Her name was Bay Lady, and she looked like she was a hundred years old. A more pitiful looking horse you have never seen in your life, but she was as sweet as she could be.

Whenever we would ride her, it was as if it took every ounce of her strength to carry my sisters and me down the road. That would all change when it was time to go back. As soon as she would get turned around, it was like being on a race horse. It was all we could do to hang on as she sprang into high gear. She would absolutely fly, trying to get back to the barn as fast as she could. It made no difference to her what got in her way. Tree branches would be slapping us in the face, and briar bushes tore at our legs as she sought the shortest route back to her stall. It makes me smile to remember how the three of us must have looked on that horse, holding on for dear life. I do so miss those times.

One summer day, daddy came home from work and said he was going to dig us a swimming pool. I remember foolishly asking him if I could swim in it that night. Daddy just smiled and got his shovel and started digging. Over the next month or so, daddy dug a pool about eight by fifteen feet, with a depth of about three feet. He built the forms and laid the filter plumbing, then poured the concrete. When it was finished, we spent almost every summer day swimming in the pool and continued using it for many summers after that. Some years later, he added on to it and made it even larger with the addition of a diving board. It makes me shake my head to think how hard daddy worked on that pool. I'm sure not many daddies would do that for their children in this day and age.

Daddy taught us all about hard work, so from an early age Terry and I did everything we could to earn our own money. If we wanted to go for ice cream or a movie, we wanted to spend our own money. Sometimes mama would take us to Parkway Village, and Terry and I would pull our red wagon from house from house selling plums. We picked them from the plum tree which housed our two board tree house and packed them into small baskets. I think we sold them for about $1.50 per basket. It would take the better part of a day to get rid of them all. Oh what young business women we were. So many memories…

But for now, my thoughts turn back to the diary resting in my lap. I can hear my grandchildren playing outside my window. They are chasing and playing the way I remember doing, and it gives me pause to think about where all the years have gone. To them, I am grandma, and like most children it is hard for them to imagine me any other way but old. In my hands, I hold the diary which proves for me it was not always so. I carefully open the diary's worn red leather cover, and once again I am young…

2

~⌒~⌒~⌒~

January 2, 1968

*...I went to school today. Came home but
didn't do anything. I washed my hair and
went to bed after watching TV a little while...*

SEEMS LIKE THE DAY WAS HARDLY EVEN
worth mentioning, and as I skim through the
entries, I find many more just as stimulating. I
suppose at the time, these mundane events
seemed worthy of the five small spaces allotted
for the day. But I suspect it was just the life of a
normal 14 year old, such as it was. Perhaps in our
own minds, we all imagine our lives at that age as
being so much more exciting. In my case, the
diary speaks differently and truthfully confronts
the reality of my life at that time.

As I continue to skim the entries, I find it
amusing to read about the childhood crushes I

had, and how easily they seemed to move on from one to the next. For sure, there was pain at the breaking of my heart, and the despair in my entries seemed as if the heartache would last forever. Looking back through the diary, it seemed like forever really never lasted that long. I turn to the entry dated…

January 26, 1968

…I went to school. Came home and sat around. About 8:00 Wayne P. & Ricky C. wanted me to go riding around with them so I did. Ricky had his arm around me. I like him…

The days flow from one to the next, and it seems yet again, this is the relationship that will surely last an eternity. At least it seemed like it would to my 14 year-old heart. At the end of the entries on each successive day, there was a heartfelt entry about Ricky in parenthesis. It would say things like, (*I still like Ricky*), or (*I like him, I wish I could see Ricky*). Then as the days progressed, the diary read, (*I love Ricky --- r.c. "n" k.t.--- hope!! it happens*).

Inevitably, the entries would begin to turn sour, for it is the way life's lessons on love are painfully learned. (W*ell, I haven't heard from Ricky in three days. I guess it's no hope for him liking me. I love him.*) With every successive turn of the page, the relationship moved closer to its ultimate conclusion…

March 12 1968

...I went to school. Came home and was ready to have class meeting and Pres. Van Hook called and said we couldn't have it. Later I went to bed. The moon was beautiful tonight. (I hardly think about Ricky anymore.)

Good for you, I thought as I read that entry, but I knew there would be other Rickys in her young future. In life there are no shortcuts around the painful times, but like all of our pasts, they help to form who we will eventually become. But not of all life's lessons are about the heart's early search for love. Some are even more powerful and just as enduring. I believe there are signs along life's road which warn us of troubled times ahead. These are sometimes hard to see without the benefit of hindsight, but they are there just the same. As I read the diary now, the sign none of us could see came on...

March 22, 1968

...I woke up this morning and didn't go to school. It had snowed 10 or 14 inches. We played in snow. Bob & Clyde came over and spent the day. We just rolled in snow. Watched TV and went to bed...

Seems like a wonderful time to have been a kid, and oh how the hot chocolate did flow. The snowfall accumulated over the next two days and approached a total of 17.5 inches. It would go down in the record books as the second largest snowfall in Memphis history. Not only was it an epic snowstorm, but it was perhaps the most colossal failure of a weather forecast of all time. On the eve of the great snowstorm, the local weatherman called for... "Occasional rain ending by the evening. Expected high of 45 deg. Low of 34 deg." I don't believe it was possible to have been more wrong. Perhaps only by General Custard, if he had said at the Battle of the Little Bighorn, "Over the hill men--I think they're friendly Indians."

It only took a few days for the snow to melt and the phone and power wires to be restored. Life seemed to be getting back to normal. But there was an even larger storm brewing, one that would have repercussions to this very day...

March 28, 1968

...I went to school. A riot started uptown today and they let some kids out of school early. Came home and Mayor Loeb made a curfew not to be out past 7:00 that night. Sat around went to bed...

Like most kids my age, I had no idea of the turmoil my hometown of Memphis was about to face. The local evening news was full of it, but as kids, we were assured it was something we needn't worry about. I can remember how mama and daddy encouraged us to leave the room and find something else to do. We listened and tried as best we could to put the images from our minds. It was of little use, for the world had reached a mountain top, and it changed for everyone in it on…

April 4, 1968

…I went to school and came home. That afternoon Dr. Martin Luther King was killed. We were at Coleman's eating when they announced his death. Mother cried. We came straight home. They put a curfew on. We slept in mother's and daddy's room that night…

The days and weeks following the shooting were filled with fear and confusion. What had been a local issue about the treatment and working conditions of the Memphis sanitation workers was now center stage for the world to see. The news was filled with protests and rallies being held all over the country; it was hard not to hear about the insanity everywhere you went. What happened that day? I'm not sure. Even now, there's still talk of conspiracies and cover ups. What I do know is how it changed this city, and of how hard it was to be 15 and caught somewhere in the middle. It was a long time before Memphis became somewhat normal again, but the wound from that single gunshot would never really heal. What a sad day for Memphis. What a sad day for all of us!

Everything changed after that day, and for the first time it seemed like all things and events revolved around race. The color of skin, something we honestly never seemed to take notice of, now became an issue. Children are a product of their environment. This is something I believe in strongly. Hate is something which is learned in the home, and like the cancer that took my daddy's life, it eats and corrupts the soul. Kids of all races began to parrot the talk around their supper tables, and it wasn't long before hatred and ignorance dripped from their mouths. It was a time of choosing, for it seemed you either had to be a hater, or a lover. It was a hard time for me, made even more so by the school I was now in.

When I was in the seventh grade, we were annexed into the city, and I had to change schools. I was now zoned for Oakhaven Middle School, which was as different as night and day from Capleville Elementary. Seventh grade can be hard enough without having to try and make new friends, or just fit in. We all know how girls at that age can form their social groups, and it is a terrible feeling to be the outsider. At my old school, everyone knew each other. The classes were small, and I liked it that way. All of the parents got along well with each other, and the mothers even got together to sew our sixth grade cheerleaders' uniforms. It was just like a great big family.

Oakhaven Middle School was different. The classes were large and the kids were standoffish, a product of the times we now found ourselves living in. Because I didn't live near the school or the neighborhoods around it, making friends was hard. Then one afternoon as I was leaving school, I saw a notice on the bulletin board announcing a cheerleading clinic. It also said open tryouts would be held the following week. I just knew this was for me, and a sure way to make lots of friends with the most popular kids in school. The diary reads…

April 17, 1968

…I went to school. I stayed after school for cheerleading clinic. I sure hope I get it. Came home and practiced and went to bed…

Even after all these years, I can still remember how it felt to be at that clinic. Girls who had been on the squad the year before wore their uniforms containing the school name and colors. I felt funny in my old gym clothes, but I held my head high and tried as hard as I could. Oh how I so wanted to get on this squad, and it showed in the entry…

April 18, 1968

…I went to school. After school I stayed for that clinic. Came home and practiced all day. Watch some TV and went to bed. (I sure wish I could get cheerleading.)…

I remember how hard I practiced those cheers, trying to get every move just right. I guess I thought if I practiced enough and put in enough energy, I would soon have one of those most desirable uniforms. But just in case effort alone wasn't enough…

April 20, 1968

…I got up about 7:00 this morning and went to cheerleading clinic. I stayed until about 2:15 and came home. I practiced cheers all day. I found a four leaf clover. I call it my good luck clover. Watched TV and went to bed…

A four-leaf clover? I never remember being superstitious as a child, but there it was. I believed this simple thing had the power to give good luck, or to keep bad luck away. I suppose I'm not alone in this belief, and there are other things people do that are just as strange. I guess I thought with the aid of my "good luck clover" I had a chance for the squad. Then I turned the page to the entry…

April 22, 1968

…I went to school. I stayed after school and tried for cheerleading squad. I didn't get it…

There is more on the lines following that, but nothing which speaks from a broken heart like the stain on the page. There is no need to wonder what it is, for I know only too well it is the remnant of a 45 year- old tear. Shed that night as I sat at my small desk, filling the diary's five small spaces. I have to remind myself that I would recover in time; my life would go on. But still, I would hold and comfort her now if I could, but of course that would be impossible. I guess it is just my maternal instincts, and before I can stop it, there is another tear on the page…

3

⌐⌐⌐⌐⌐

I AM STARTLED BACK TO THE PRESENT by a knock on my door. It is my granddaughter Timeri, politely asking if she can go to the movies with some of her friends. At 14, she is the oldest of my five grandchildren, and I invite her in. I ask all the prerequisite questions, the same ones her mother Brittney would ask and send her on her way with a reminder, "to be careful." I am taken aback by how grown she looks, and of how much she reminds me of my daughter at that age. It seems like I just turned around and Brittney was grown, and it was only yesterday I held Timeri in my arms as she gazed upon this world. Time has a way of passing, and I wonder where all the years have gone, and of how they could have passed so quickly. Like toppling dominoes, life has no rewind button, but instead seems only to be stuck on fast forward. Now, more than ever, I find myself searching for the button which will pause, or at least slow time's steady progression.

As Timeri waits outside with one of her friends, I can hear the giggles of their conversation and know it can mean only one thing. Boys! I fear she may be as boy crazy as I was at that age, but the times seem much different now. Society has changed much about its value system; it seems like the kids are constantly bombarded on the internet and TV with a constant theme of sex. She is wiser to the ways of the world than I ever was at that age, and probably several more years beyond. It worries me at times, but I realize she has been raised well, and I trust completely in the character of her heart.

When her friend's mother arrives to take them, I wave to her from the porch, and then they are gone. As they turn the corner out of sight, I feel a pang in my heart as I briefly remember my teenage years. I recall the feelings of being out of school, and the seemingly endless summer days that lay before me. But it is one summer in particular that once again draws my attention to the diary…

June 6, 1968

…Got up and heard Robert Kennedy died. Mother cried, and I went to the beach and swam. Came back to cabin. Daddy and I went and walked the beach. Daddy couldn't understand what was wrong with the world. Came home and got ready and went to The Hangout. I was asked to dance by a boy that was a surfer. He kissed me for the first time.

Ever since I can remember, our family spent two weeks in June and two weeks in July vacationing in Gulf Shores. We stayed in a cabin daddy had helped build for mother's brother Wallace, and it was right on the bay. I was probably about five when they built it. It occupied about three or four lots on what is now called Orange Beach. I remember the concrete floor and cinder block walls, and the screened-in porch on three sides. The cabin only had one bedroom, so we slept on foldout couches in the living room, and cots on the porch. Oh, how I can remember falling asleep to the sounds of the rhythmic waves, the cool night breezes, and the soothing calls of the ocean birds. It was a paradise, and I could have lived there forever.

That year's vacation was forever marred by the Kennedy assassination which visibly upset both of my parents. The mood for the most part was somber, and my parents worried if this killing would also have long term repercussions. As kids, we probably spent more time alone that vacation than was usual, but we still had fun.

During the day, we swam and fished in the ocean and lounged on blankets in the warm sun. The sand on the beach was amazing, and over the years we probably built a thousand castles or more, only to watch them be reclaimed, once again, by the sea. At night, with flashlights and sand pails in hand, we searched the shallow surf for blue crabs. Sometimes we spent the evenings sitting near fires built of driftwood, toasting marshmallows and listening to ghost stories, until well into the night.

On some of the nights during our stay, my sisters and I would walk down the road to a place called The Hangout. At that time there wasn't too much development in Orange Beach, and you either had to go into Gulf Shores, or cross the bridge into Florida to find much of anything. The Hangout was just down the road. It was just a small place with a restaurant, and somewhere the local kids would go at night to just hang out. There was a room in the back overlooking the surf, and the kids would just sit around talking and dancing to the juke box music. I loved it there.

I suppose looking back on it now I thought it was probably the greatest place ever to live. I'm sure most of the kids who did live there were thinking the exact opposite and couldn't wait to someday leave that small town. I guess, like always, it just depends on what side of the fence you're on. From my side, it couldn't be more perfect.

On the night of this entry, my sisters and I were in the back listening to music. It was getting late, and I knew we would have to go back to the cabin soon. I could see the paper lantern lights on the porch swaying gently in the evening breeze; they seemed to be moving rhythmically to the music. Boys and girls were dancing slowly around the floor, and then a boy came over to me and asked if I wanted to dance.

I had noticed him several times that evening and thought he was cute, but he totally caught me by surprise. It was the first time I had ever been asked to dance, at least by someone who did not know me. On top of all that, he was a surfer, and I thought being one was the coolest thing ever. It was like a dream when he took my hand and led me to the dance floor. The song that was playing ended, and then Otis Redding came on the jukebox singing "(Sittin' On) The Dock Of The Bay." He took me into his arms and we began to dance. Neither one of us knew how, so it was mostly just swaying slowly and moving in small circles. There was the occasional stepping on the feet, either his or mine, but it was still magical to me.

When that song ended, we danced a few more times, and then I told him we had to leave. He asked if we were going to come back tomorrow night, but I told him we were leaving for home in the morning. Then, before I knew what was happening, he pressed me hard against him and kissed me on the lips. It was nothing like I had imagined my first kiss would be like. Perhaps my expectations were too high, for I thought it would be more like Rhett Butler kissing Scarlett in "Gone with the Wind." It was nothing like that.

He pressed his lips so hard against mine it felt like I was kissing a kneecap. He frantically tried to slip his tongue into my mouth, and I wasn't having any of that. Perhaps if I had been more prepared, it might have been a better experience. That and the fact that his breath smelled like Cheerios was also a bit of a turnoff. Still, I suppose it was somewhat romantic, and I left that night thinking I had found yet another boyfriend. In my mind, I thought we would see each other every time we came back to the beach. Although we later spent many summers there, I never saw him again. Sometimes I still remember that first dance and kiss, especially when I'm eating a bowl of Cheerios.

Over the years, I took my kids and grandchildren every summer to the little cabin on the beach. Their memories of the place have become just as etched as mine. Sometimes we would stay a few weeks, sometimes longer. I never grew tired of watching them play in the same stretch of surf I had so enjoyed, although the area was now completely different. Houses were now tightly packed along the beach, and there were major condominiums going up everywhere.

About 10 years ago, my cousins sold the small cabin my daddy had helped to build--so many years ago. A large home now occupies the space, and it must be valued in the millions. As nice as it is, I wouldn't trade it for the little cabin which once looked over this isolated stretch of beach. No home, no matter how nice, could ever replace the memories of long summer days, or my first kiss on the dance floor of The Hangout.

I close the diary once again and remember how naïve I was at that age. I remember how confused and scared I was when I was 12 and had my first period. I was not prepared, and it was something I had yet to discuss with my mother. Thankfully, I had my older sister Terry to help me in times of need. In many ways she was like a mother to me and always seemed to be looking out for me. She filled an important role in my life, and if I didn't thank her enough growing up, I do so now. She helped me more than she will ever know.

As for my mother, she had five older siblings, and two younger. Her mother died when she was 12, and it was very hard for her. Raised by older brothers, she had no one she could turn to, and no one to help her with the physical changes she was going through. I was always grateful for the help she would give me, but I knew it had been very hard on her as a child. Her memories of that time in her life are not pleasant, but in the end it would help to shape the strong person she would become. I don't believe I ever wanted to be anything else but a momma and raise children of my own. I am, in fact, with five children of my own, and I don't believe I could have done it without her. I grew strong in her shadow and love her so very much.

Daddy was the youngest of eight children and was born with a twin sister. They did not look the same, nor were they similar in their personalities. Daddy was very outgoing and had a giant personality. He was always quick with a joke, or a great big smile, and there wasn't anything he wouldn't do to help someone out. His sister was more refined and didn't seem to project her strong personality the way daddy did. As they grew older, they drifted further apart, and their relationship began to strain. Towards the end of her life, daddy tried to mend the void between them. While it did not happen on this earth, I'm sure they are together once again in heaven. That is a prayer which I pray.

I know on this earth, she couldn't have had a better brother. When daddy was in the ninth grade, he quit school so he could work and help to support the family. After Pearl Harbor, daddy and his brother joined the army and went to fight in the war. Before he left, he moved maw and paw, (that's what we called them growing up), to Memphis and bought them a house. For four years, he sent his Army pay home for their mortgage and living expenses. I should think there aren't too many sons or brothers who would sacrifice so much for their family.

He never seemed to expect anything from anybody and always just seemed to want to help others. Maw and paw both lived into their nineties and daddy cared for them both until the day they died. When paw became ill and wasn't able to do for himself, daddy would stay with him before going to work in the morning. On those days, he would shave his face with a straight razor and make sure his hair was neatly combed. I still have the razor daddy used. I can't hold it now without thinking of them both. Daddy was always doing something for the family, and that is what made it so perfect when he met mother.

Daddy was ten years older than mother, and he was her absolute soul mate. He had spent his life doing for others, and after they were married, he did the same for her. There was nothing mother could have wished for that daddy didn't try to provide for her. It was just his nature to look out for the wants and needs of others, and he truly required nothing in return. One October for his birthday, we planned a small surprise birthday party for him. Nothing fancy--just a few friends and family over for cake and ice cream, and a few small gifts. You would have thought we had given daddy the moon.

Slipped within the pages of the diary is a handwritten note from daddy. I found it on my desk the day after the party, and I know it must have taken him some time to write it. While his penmanship is very shaky, and his grammar wouldn't score well on a school paper, I don't think anything could be more beautiful to me. I shall share it with you now, just the way it is written, so you can better know my father...

Dear Kathy

You don't know how much it meant to me to have a daughter to do. so much to have me a birthday party. I know you realy dun a lot to have a party like we had. It means so much to me to know I have daughters that love me enough to do this for me. I am realy proud of you I cant figure why God has been so good to me giving me daughters like you and a wife like I've got, but Im thankful for all of you.

I love you so much

Daddy

This simple handwritten letter speaks volumes about my daddy, but I feel like the only thing he got wrong was that God must have blessed us with him. I do miss him so.

Terry graduated from high school that year of the surprise party and would begin college at Memphis State in the fall. Daddy gave her a car for her graduation present, and he spent three hundred and fifty dollars on it. As was daddy's way of doing things, he would later spend the same exact amount on mine and Karen's car. One thing about daddy, he would never be accused of showing favoritism. Terry got an older model Mercury Comet, and I'm not even sure what year it was. I do remember it was white, and daddy painted the roof blue to look like it had a vinyl top.

Although it wasn't the nicest car in town, Terry was very proud of it. She added small touches to the inside and put her personal stamp on it. There were surfer feet for the gas pedal and headlight dimmer switch, and an eight ball was fashioned for a shifter knob. Later the car became known simply as the "Vomit Comet," because of how it looked, but we still went everywhere in it. There were many trips to football games, and to the local McDonalds afterwards to just hang out and get a bite to eat. At times it seemed a little out of place, but perhaps never more than when it passed a gated tree-lined drive, that wound to the home of a king…

4

꩜꩜꩜꩜

MY ATTENTION IS ONCE AGAIN DRAWN to the entries, and I skim through the summer of 1969. There is much written within the spaces that screams of boredom and monotony, and to say otherwise would simply be untrue. There are entries about the occasional date, or trip to the movies, with some boy or another. Most of the boys are older, and it seems most are friends or acquaintances of Terry's. As it turned out, many of the friends I would have in high school were because of Terry. She was always so outgoing, it just seemed natural to her to socialize and make friends. For me, it always seemed to be a struggle. I would have to describe myself back then as shy and quiet. Sometimes it seems like I didn't learn how to speak up for myself until I had children of my own.

In July of that year, I started working at my first real job. I had been babysitting for many years, but this was a steady job in the church preschool. I worked from three to six in the afternoons during the week and kept the children until their parents showed up to take them home. The children were all younger than five, so it was mostly just supervising their play when the teacher left for the day. There were some precious ones under the age of two, and I cherished holding and caring for them the most. It only seemed to reinforce my desire to be a mother, and I could think of nothing I could ever want more. There are entries about one particular baby or another, and of how sweet they were to hold, but I never seemed to have a favorite. I guess that's just how it would be with my own children.

During this summer of my 16th year, there are many entries about a dear friend of our family named Redd. I suppose we have all known at least one person like him, someone who cares about others without ever expecting anything in return-- that was Redd. There is a special place in my heart for him, and I smile when I remember the way he looked. He was tall and rail thin, and his hair was shock red. He always wore it in a flattop hair style, and it stood a full two inches high above his head. He had a long thin nose and always seemed to have a cigar in his mouth. We never said anything to him about it, but we thought he looked just like Ichabod Crane.

While physically he was as thin as a willow shoot, inside, his heart was the size of Texas. I don't believe I've ever met a more caring and helpful man in my whole life. He worked with daddy at the tire plant, but he spent so much time with us, he seemed more like family. He ate supper with us about three or four times a week, and I suppose looking back on it, he didn't seem to have much of a home life. He was never married and lived his whole life with his mother, taking care of her and seeing to her needs. I think sometimes he just needed out of his mother's house for awhile, so he would come to ours just to get away. In many ways, I think he was just bored with life and didn't want to sit around with his mother all the time. He always wanted to try new things, and it was his spirit for life that I remember the most.

One year, Redd bought a couple of small motorcycles just because he wanted to ride. He kept them at our house, and we used to ride those bikes with him all the time. We rode them all around the industrial park close to our house and in the woods behind it. It was so much fun. I remember riding as fast as that little bike would go, and of how the wind would make my eyes water down the sides of my cheeks. As I close my eyes now, I can almost feel the wind in my face and can faintly hear the roar of that engine as the throttle twisted in my hand. We used to take turns riding the bikes and played games of follow the leader as we rode through the woods. I know my grandchildren would have a hard time believing I ever rode one, but there was a time it was so. Those were the best of times, and all because Redd wanted to try something. He was always doing something like that--just because.

One summer he wanted to try photography, so he bought an expensive backdrop and a couple of very nice cameras. He used to take our pictures for practice; I still have a few of the better ones that turned out. On another occasion, he bought a bunch of Plaster of Paris molds to try his hand at art. I remember he had some that looked like eagles, and when the plaster dried we painted and finished them in gold leaf. We would sell them to anyone that would buy one, and I'm pretty sure he never kept any of the money for himself.

Redd was as close to family as you can get, and he went on many of our vacation trips. There were trips to the mountains, the beach, and one summer we even went to California together. Then one Sunday, Redd went to church with us. He wasn't familiar with the Lord; in fact, I don't think he had ever set foot in a church before. Daddy felt like it was important for him to learn about the ways of the Bible, and he went a few more times with us. Then one Sunday, it was suggested by a church member that he lead everyone in prayer. I remember how mad daddy got at the congregation's insensitivity for putting that kind of pressure on him. Redd was somewhat shy around strangers, and I think it embarrassed him terribly to be the focus of everyone's attention. He quit going to church with us after that, and to my knowledge, I don't think he ever went to a service again.

Although he would never be a regular in the Lord's house, I believe he always had the Lord's work in his heart. He was generous to a fault, and he never asked, or wanted anything in return. He was always doing something for others, and at times, it seemed like he was always bringing us something. Sometimes it was candy, on other times it might be flowers or gifts, and it was always--just because. In the back of my dresser drawer is a special gift from Redd, one I have cherished for all these years. The small box is worn from age, but inside is the gift he gave to me for my 16th birthday--a pair of small ruby earrings with gold posts. They are as dear to me now as they ever were.

As I hold them in my hands, they take me back to another time and place, and I say a short prayer for Redd. He died quite a few years ago, and it still tears at my heart to think of the way he left this world. We didn't even know he had died until days after, but that was the way Redd wanted it. He never wanted to bother or be a burden to anyone. After he was diagnosed with a rare form of cancer, he checked into a hospital without ever saying a word. He died alone, wasted away to skin and bones, and it makes me sad to think about him that way.

A knock at my door snaps me back to the present. It is my youngest daughter Tatum. I invite her in, and as she sits on the bed beside me, I show her the earrings in the worn box. I remind her of how they were given to me, and by whom, and I put them back in the drawer. She is a lot like me and has never been one to go overboard with jewelry. I have a few precious pieces, as does my daughter Tatum, and that is enough for me. I suppose the beads which Elvis gave to me one summer evening are among the most prized of all that I have. They have no worth as it pertains to precious stones, but he gave them to me--just plain, ordinary me--but I shall treasure them forever.

I talk with my daughter about the life I once had, and lived, in what now seems so very long ago. I show her an entry in my diary about Aunt Ruby and can see by the way she seems to look at nothing in particular that she can remember. Aunt Ruby was daddy's oldest sister, and she all but raised him when he was young. She was married for a long time, but the Lord had never blessed her with children. My grandparents died when I was very young, and Aunt Ruby was like a grandmother to us when we grew up. We used to stay at her house all the time, and she spent every holiday and birthday with us throughout those years. I remember the beautiful corsages she would bring for us at Christmas and on our birthdays, and even though she wasn't, I couldn't imagine a more perfect grandmother.

Aunt Ruby was a longtime employee at Lowenstein's department store, in Whitehaven, where she managed the ladies' hats and wigs department. Terry started working there when she was 16, and the summer of 1969 would be her last. That summer was a period of transition for both of us, for she would be attending Memphis State in the fall, and the beginning of my high school years stretched endlessly before me. I would take Terry's job when she started school at summer's end, and like Terry, I would work there throughout my high school years. By the time I started working there, I knew just about everything there was to know about the place, just from hanging around there so much with Terry. I would go over there after school and just wait for her to get finished so we could go do something afterwards. Sometimes I would help her with inventory or stocking, just so we could get out of there faster.

Most of the time, after she would close for the evening, we would just ride around in the Vomit Comet. Sometimes we would go to the high school football or basketball games, or maybe to the movies. On other evenings, we would drive around to see what everyone else was doing. For the most part, it wasn't much of anything, and we would end up just driving around. These evenings would usually end up with us hanging out with the kids at the McDonalds. At times, the things we did after Terry got off work seemed packed with excitement and fun, while other nights were a complete bore and a total waste of time. Looking back on it now, I guess you never knew what the evening held, but I guess you didn't want to take a chance and miss something.

As I hold the diary in my hand, I am flooded with the memories of the summer of 1969. I draw a deep breath as the emotions wash over me, and it is as if I had somehow traveled back in time. The feelings and sensations are fresh in my mind, as if only yesterday, yet I know many years have passed since my summer of transition. Somehow, the dream of time travel has stuck in my head, and it makes me wonder what I would do if it were possible. I am content in my life, with a fine husband, five grown children, and five grandchildren whom I love more than I can express. Still, if the well of wishes that could grant such a thing were before me now--would I dare? Would the coin slip freely from my hand, or would I fold it tightly back into my palm? I suppose it is a silly thought, for such a thing is not possible. I know the only way to go back in time is to turn the page my hand now rests upon. Hesitating for a moment, I realize the only way for me to go forward is to go back. With a flood of emotions, I am 16 once again, and I turn to the next entry. Call it fate or Karma, if that is your belief, but my life was forever changed on…

July 2, 1969

…Terry got off work and we rode by Elvis' house and he was out there. We parked and everyone was around him. We finally got up there close to him and Terry asked him to kiss her. He did, and when he was raising up he reached around my neck and frenched me. Then he pulled me to him and frenched me again. Terry and I backed off, but he kept looking at us and smiling at us so we figured we would try to get up there again. We watched him for awhile, and every once in a while he would say something just to us. He had on a pin (Tell it like it is) and I said what does that say? Terry said it and he heard her and said you can have it. I was standing there looking around and he told a woman shhh and bent over and kissed me on

*the neck. I was surprised. He told her I
didn't ask for it; he just felt like doing it. I
would be standing there and he would just
bend over and kiss me real good and long.
Before he got down off the stand a woman
was having her picture made with him. I lost
my balance a little and sort of fell on him
and he grabbed my hand with one of his
hands and put the other on my waist and
squeezed me. Then he held my hand the
whole time he had his picture made with the
woman and it took a long time. He would
squeeze my hand in his and press it against
his leg. Before he got down he said wait a
minute and I'll get down between you two
and I said ok. He got down and a guard had
his arm before he could put it around
Terry's waist but he already had one arm
around me and had told the guard to let go
and he squeezed me real tight against him
and frenched me for a long time. I quit and
he pulled me up again and would not let me
go, and he did it again. After this he just kept
on. Then he kissed Terry once. Everyone was
pushing trying to get to him but we were the
only ones that he would let up there. We
walked with him to his golf cart. Everyone
else crowded around but we walked further
into the yard and stood in the shadow of a
tree. Finally he told everyone to please move
back. He took off in his cart and when he got
in front of us Terry yelled Elvis and he
looked around. I just stood there and he*

turned off his motor and said "Come here" to me. I walked over and he put his arm around my neck and frenched me good for a long time then said by and drove off. We left and came home and told mother and Karen then went to bed. (I had red marks above my lips where he kissed me so much).

I can vividly remember that night, and of how my hand shook as I wrote in the diary about what had happened. I must have pinched myself a hundred times to see if I was dreaming, but I only had to look at the whisker burns on my face to know it was true. I must admit, at the time, I didn't really know that much about Elvis, nor was I all that familiar with his music or movies. One thing I did know was that he was the most famous person in Memphis, and without a doubt the most famous I would probably ever meet. He had made my heart flutter, that was for sure, and no one I had ever met had done that before. Sleep came hard for me that night, and my thoughts were filled with Elvis. Why me? I couldn't understand why he had fixated on me over the hundred other women who were hanging on the fence. I drifted to sleep wondering if I would ever see him again. I wouldn't have to wait long.

July 3, 1969

...Got up and sat around. Terry and I did running for mother. Came home and got ready to go and see Elvis. I knew he wouldn't come out. But!! (on paper)...

I was so afraid all day that we wouldn't get to see him. We got there and Terry made me stand right at crack where he could see me. When guard opened the gate I was the first one in. He saw me and said, "Hi Baby, remember last night?" We were the only ones that stood on the stump with him and one of the guards. I sat between his legs and he kept saying stay there and don't leave me. I got up after awhile and stood behind him. Finally he said, "I've got to go," and he started getting off the stump. I told Terry we haven't got our picture made yet. He heard me and told the guard to take us up further into the yard. Everyone was listening and we felt so big. The police made a path for us to walk through. We walked on up into the yard while he waited for all the people to move for his cart. We stood and talked to Mr. Presley while waiting and Elvis came up there and started talking about all those girls wanting to kiss him. The police were wanting to come up and meet him and he said, "Y'all sit down and wait until after they leave." He joked around with the police and with us for awhile. He kept looking at me and winking and when the police were fixing to come up there, I was sitting on the edge of his cart and he looked and winked at me. Then he leaned over and kissed me for a long time. (frenched) He asked me how old I was and I told him I was 18. Terry told him that I was barely 16 and he told Terry he had dated girls my age before.

47

He got through kissing me and said in my ear, "I love the way you kiss." He kept smiling at me and I would get tickled and just smile back. Finally we kissed him goodbye and said we had to go. Terry said something about us going home and watching the movie and he said, "It's not as good as the one going on here, is it?" We were at the bottom of the hill and someone started calling my name. I turned around and he was running down the hill hollering my name. We turned around and he walked right up to me and didn't say a thing but just started kissing me. We kissed for about five minutes and he was grunting the whole time. He stood holding on to me and asked, "Can I have Kathy for tonight?" Terry said, "I don't think mother would like that." He said, "Don't tell her. Tell her she is at a slumber party or something." Then he started kissing me again. Once he put his tongue way down my throat. He kept rubbing my stomach and scratching my back while he was kissing me. Terry said, "Well, we better go," and we just kept kissing. He looked up and told Terry to be quiet and shook his fist at her. Then we started kissing again. We kissed about 30 minutes and he squeezed me so tight I could feel his breathing and everything. Then he looked at me and told me I was some girl and gave me some beads he had on. Then he said, "Boy Kathy, you have got my heart beating so fast." Then we kissed again and he kept kissing me on the neck and temple. He told Terry that he wasn't griping and to stay a little longer. Then he kissed me for about five minutes and whispered into my ear goodbye. We turned and walked off and he waved goodbye. He got my phone number and said he would call me. Came home and went to bed.

Reading this entry once again has made my heart swoon and my head spin, much as it did the night it happened. Strong emotions are flowing over me in waves, and to quell the memories, I must turn this page…

5

꙲꙲꙲꙲

I CLOSE THE DIARY FOR NOW.

I can't sit in my room all night reminiscing. I have dinner to prepare. My oldest son Dax and his wife Lisa are coming to dine with us and bringing my grandchildren Haddon and Phoebe. They live across the road from us, not much more than a quarter mile, so I see them quite regularly. Still, I enjoy their company very much, and it's good to have family around the table.

Conversation flows freely as we eat and talk about our day, and the grandkids tell me all about what they are doing in school. Haddon is 12 and Phoebe is 9, and their faces remind me of angels as I listen to them recant their day. Over time, the evening has a way of passing, and it was no different on this night. The kids had homework, and Dax was tired from work, so they kissed me goodbye and left. As I cleaned up the table from the meal, my mind kept drifting back to the diary. It seemed strange that something I hadn't even thought about for years now had such a strong pull on me. Then as I was putting the dishes in the sink, I found a piece of gum stuck to the edge of Haddon's plate. He was saving it for later, and it made me think of another piece of gum that was once saved.

Inside the diary entry for that July night when I first met Elvis is a piece of gum. It's folded carefully into the corner of the page, and the inscription reads, *"This gum has really had his tongue on it."* I don't remember what kind it was, (probably Juicy Fruit if I had to guess), but I have to cover my mouth to keep from laughing. What was I thinking? I suppose it is kind of gross, but I was just 16, and at that time I guess I thought it was something that needed to be saved. Whatever the reason, it is still pressed onto the page, like a seal of dripped candle wax, from a long time ago.

With the dishes done and the kitchen cleaned up, I drift back to my bedroom, and, once again, find the diary in my hand. I turn carefully to the days immediately after meeting Elvis and am reminded of the disappointment and confusion that time had once brought to me. I couldn't understand why I hadn't heard from him. I knew he had my number. I remember how he had written it down on a scrap of paper in his golf cart. Still, the phone did not ring. In the days immediately after our encounter with him, I can remember imploring Terry to drive slowly every time we would pass Graceland. I would crane my neck out the window of the comet, searching the grounds looking for him. He was never there.

I skim through day after day, reading the entries on the five narrow lines, and they are filled with disappointment. My life had returned to the boring and mundane; it seemed to go on that way day after day. There are entries about work at the church daycare, or babysitting someone's child. Other entries are about movies, and shopping, and coming home and watching TV. All of these excitement filled days are concluded with, *"Went to bed."*

What the diary does not convey are the restless and sleepless nights filled with the thoughts of Elvis. Night after night, my thoughts and dreams were overflowing with him. I constantly replayed every second in my mind, when he had kissed and held me so tight in his arms. At times, it all just seemed like a dream--a dream so wonderful and vivid, that it never seemed to stray very far from my heart. I guess that was the problem. I was just 16 and couldn't seem to grasp why I hadn't heard from him. Perhaps what I hoped for bordered on the impossible, but lately, the impossible seemed to be coming true. I watched breathlessly, along with the rest of the world, when what was once only a dream, became reality.

July 19, 1969

...Got up and Terry and I went at 8:00 to take inventory at Lowenstein's. I worked all day with Jim Honea. Terry worked in china and I worked in lotions. Came home and watched as men landed on the moon for the first time in history. Mother cried and everyone was amazed. Went to bed at 1:00...

What a time that was. I can remember the news reports that followed, and of how the papers were filled with articles of American pride and accomplishment. It was a great time in our nation's history and only seemed to prove what we could do when we all worked together. Back then, it seemed as if everyone pulled on the rope of progress in the same direction. Then, it was possible to do the impossible. Now it seems like we just pull the rope from opposite ends, going nowhere and accomplishing nothing. I fear it is a sad time for our country, and in turn, the rest of the world. How I wish it could be different for the sake of my grandchildren's future.

I skim through the rest of July's entries, searching for more thoughts and memories of Elvis, but they seem to be waning. The boredom of my life had returned in spades, and I felt, once again, how it must have been for the fabled Cinderella. I had read the story hundreds of times for my children and knew firsthand how she must have felt. I had experienced how wonderful it was, to be center stage at the most glamorous of balls, dancing in the arms of a handsome prince. Looking deeply into his eyes, and feeling the brush of his lips upon my face, only to have it all end with the toll of a clock, returning once again to the plain and ordinary life she had always known. I was no princess, and there would be no slipper of glass for me to try on. It was only a children's story, and after page after page in the diary, the entries seemed resigned to that fact. I was only feeling sorry for myself, but there were other things happening, especially in the state of Mississippi, that were much worse.

August 16, 1969

...Went to Sunday school. Came home and went to rush parties and bowling session. Came home and went to bed after watching TV. There is a terrible hurricane going on...

Camille. That was her name, and I don't believe there has ever been another to match her fury. I remember the reports on her progress as she neared our coastal shores, and of how she had surprised everyone with her wrath. I think what astounded the weather forecasters so much was how much strength she had gathered so close to shore. She was without mercy when she made landfall with winds near 200 mph or perhaps more. No instruments survived to tell for sure. In her wake, 259 lives would be taken before she made her way back to the sea from where she had come. Her damage in lives and property was almost without equal, and she left our nation filled with destruction and sorrow. It was a sad time indeed. Still, in the bleakness of that night, there is a small entry written in the border of the page for that night. It is only three words...*watched Elvis special...*

I couldn't believe, between the hurricane reports, I was watching him on TV. He was singing somewhere in Las Vegas, and it was amazing. This was the first time I had ever seen him perform, and it was dreamlike watching him on stage. Women were going crazy, pulling at their hair, and clamoring for him to touch them or begging for a piece of his clothing. I knew he was famous in Memphis, but I had no idea he was just as famous somewhere else. As I watched him sing his songs, I was reminded of how Mr. Presley had told me he was going out of town for awhile. I had totally forgotten, and my heart was instantly lifted. I still had a chance, and I went to bed with dreams of Elvis, once again, and wondered if he might be singing to me.

The rest of that summer of 1969 passed without much fanfare. There are entries about work, or about how a boy had tried to hold my hand at the movies, but it all seems so bland. I started high school that fall and remember how much I never really cared for it. I tried to get involved in school activities, including pledging a sorority. When Terry was in high school, she had been very active in Sigma Alpha Delta, so I thought it was something I should try. There were lots of popular girls in it, including the cheerleaders, and I thought it would help me fit in. Besides, some of Terry's younger friends were still in it, so I already knew most of them.

Rush lasted for six weeks, and it seemed filled with stupid things. Early on, I could tell the sorority life was not for me, but I wanted to give it a chance for Terry. She had worked hard to get me in, and I just didn't want to let her down. Most of the things we had to do seemed foolish, but I did them anyway just to get in. One day, in front of a packed cafeteria, I had to stand and sing a song. I couldn't tell anyone why I was doing it, and it was the most embarrassing thing I had ever done. On another occasion, after a football game, another pledge and I had to act like fools at the McDonalds. Everyone was looking at us like we were crazy, as we ate sandwiches made only of ketchup and mustard.

When rush was over, mother was nice enough to let us have our initiation ceremony at the house. I remember what a mess it was when we were done and can still recall how hard it was to clean it all back up again the next day. During the initiation, we had mustard and honey poured all over our heads, and it got on everything. By the light of candles, we were made to bite a raw onion and had to eat a hot pepper, along with other things equally as stupid. When it was all over, everyone had to take a shower in my bathroom, and you can just imagine the mess it made. I thought the whole thing was dumb, but I so wanted to fit in, I did it just the same.

Later in the school year, we started having meetings about once a month. They were held at different members' houses and were mostly about making plans for some fundraiser or another. To raise money for the sorority, we held car washes or had school dances. They were mostly on the weekends, but sometimes we sold baked goods at a basketball or football game during the week. For the most part, I didn't want to go to the meetings. They would always end up with the girls smoking cigarettes and talking about some silly boy. I was working most nights and weekends at Lowenstein's then, and along with my schoolwork, my schedule was pretty full. This just seemed like such a waste of time.

One night, a meeting was scheduled, and everyone was supposed to be there. I had to work that night, and by the time I got off the meeting would have been just about over. I was tired and didn't want to have to break my neck hurrying to someone's house, just to watch girls smoke and talk about boys. I didn't go, and at the next month's meeting, the sorority wanted to fine me five dollars for the meeting I had missed. It was to be their new policy, and I would be fined five dollars in the future for every meeting that I missed. I think that was the last straw for me, and I decided right then to drop out. I think it was the first thing I had ever quit in my life.

About a month later, I got my sorority pin in the mail. I felt bad because mother had spent a lot of money on it. The one I picked out had a small solitary diamond and a pearl, along with the blue stone in the center with the sorority's initials scribed into it. I loved the pin, but at the same time knew I couldn't wear it. I took it to the jewelers and had him replace the blue stone with a fake diamond of about the same size. I've worn it quite a few times over the years, and as I hold it in my hands, I can still remember the first time as if it were only yesterday.

December 20, 1969

...Got up and didn't go to school. Mother and I cleaned house all day. I went and got my

hair fixed in curls and came home and got ready for Ralph Johnson to come and pick me up for winter formal...

This was my first formal, and the entry from that night is a full page in length. It seems strange to me as I now hold it in my hand, how I could ever think it could be summed up in so few words. I knew all about the dance from the school newspaper, but it was now late into October, less than two months away, and still no one had asked me to go. Then a boy in one of my classes asked me to the dance, and I jumped at the invitation.

After that, I remember frantically searching for just the right dress, and I probably went to every dress shop in town before I found it. It was a floor length dress made of red velvet and had a cream colored chiffon neck line that fit me just perfect. It was the most beautiful dress I had ever worn. It cost more than I had intended to spend, so I put it on layaway and made weekly payments on it. If all went according to plan and I put most of my paycheck into the dress, I would get it out of layaway with two weeks to spare. Everything seemed to be going perfectly, but as we all know, that is the time for things to turn horribly bad.

It was between classes one day--I'm not even sure I remember when--that my date for the dance cancelled on me. I was too shocked to even hear his explanation, much less remember it, but I'm sure it must have been pretty lame. I was just dumbfounded. As I watched him walk away, I told myself I didn't need to go to a stupid dance anyway and almost convinced myself it was true. Then I remembered my dress. I still had it in layaway, with only a few payments left. The dress was so beautiful, and I had imagined myself at the dance wearing it. I don't know how I kept from crying at school that day, but the tears flowed freely once I got to work.

When one of the older girls I worked with saw my tears, I confided in her what had happened at school that day. She was aware of the dress I had planned to wear and knew how much I was looking forward to my first formal. After she suggested several terrible things that boy could do, and where he could go, she came up with a simple plan. I would just have to ask a boy to go with me. I thought there was no way I could do that, but the more I played it over in my mind, the more I decided to do it. I was so nervous, and it was more than a little awkward, but I asked Ralph the next day. I was so relieved when he said he would go with me.

I knew him pretty well and felt comfortable around him, but I had no romantic ideas about him. When he came to pick me up, he was dressed in a dark suit and had a pink corsage for me to wear. Mother pinned it on for me, and Terry pinned his carnation on his lapel. It seemed like we posed for a hundred pictures before we finally left. Ralph practically broke his neck racing for the door to open it for me; it was all so sweet. We picked up another couple on the way to the dance, and it didn't seem so awkward with other people in the car.

Later, the dance was pretty much as I had imagined. We spent a lot of time sitting at the table, but we also slow danced quite a few times. I saw my original date a few times, dancing with a much more popular girl than me. At first, I was so angry I couldn't see straight. Then I thought, I wouldn't let him spoil my evening and just never made eye contact with him. I made up my mind I would have a better time than he would and believe in the end I probably did.

The evening was later summed up in the entry on the page…

> *…He followed me to the gate and then to the door. I unlocked it and he came in. We just stood there looking at each other like dummies. Then he said, "Well, I guess I'd better get going." Then as he was walking out the door, he spun around quickly and kissed me on the cheek. I thought he was going to kiss me again, but he didn't. I told him to be careful going home and closed the door…*

That is how the entry of my first formal dance ends, and I suppose I wondered if that was how it always was. I remember how I felt afterwards and wondered how it would have been if I had gone with someone I really had feelings for. I wondered what the dance would have been like, with a prince once again in my arms. As it turned out, I wouldn't have to wait very long…

MY FARAWAY DREAMS OF A DANCE long ago are interrupted by the ringing telephone. It is my younger sister Karen who wants me to go to the movies with her. We are closer now than when we were kids. I suppose it's because the four years difference in our ages is not such a big deal anymore. When we were younger, she had her own friends and her own life, and we just always seemed to be going in different directions. Maybe that's how it is in most families when there are some years between siblings.

I declined her invitation to the show, and after a few minutes of conversation, I hung up the phone. While the movie she wanted to see sounded good, I just couldn't bring myself to go. I'm not phobic about germs or anything, but I must admit, I don't relish the thought of sitting in a theater chair. I would have to bring a clean sheet to cover the chair with, just to be somewhat comfortable. Without a doubt, I would need a bottle of hand sanitizer in my purse, if I thought I would have touch something. Thinking about how I would look in that theater seat, draped in a sheet, frantically rubbing my hands with sanitizer, makes me smile. I wasn't always that way, and there are many entries in my diary when I jumped at the chance to go to the movies. On many of those occasions, the invitation came from Elvis.

I don't know how long he had been doing it, or when it had started, but he used to rent the old Memphian Theater on Cooper Street. It was always late at night, and the movies would roll until early in the morning. I won't presume to understand the reason why he did it, but I suppose it was so he wouldn't be mobbed. Seeing him perform on television had opened my eyes to how popular he was to his fans. I guess this was a place where he felt comfortable, and where he could just try and fit in. It seems like a sad way to have lived, and I now realize how isolated his life must have been. I suppose at 16 the world just looked different to me, and everything about him seemed to sparkle. Even in the darkness of the theater, he seemed to shine brighter than the screen. Perhaps that is why I can't remember a single movie I ever watched with him.

Most late night screenings consisted of about two or three movies, always the ones Elvis wanted to watch. If he didn't like a particular movie for one reason or another, he would have it stopped after only about thirty minutes, and he would have another started. Whenever Terry and I would go with him, it always seemed like the same twenty or so people were there. I knew some of their names then, and a few more now, but it never seemed important to ever meet them at the time. For those of you who know everything about Elvis' life, you know their names and their stories. Most of them are no longer with us, and there is nothing written in my diary about them that I can add. I only know that wherever Elvis was, this group of men would not be far away.

The only man in this entourage that Terry and I really knew was Charlie Hodge. He was the one who more or less told Terry the unwritten rules of the theater, and we were determined to follow them and not make anyone mad. Charlie told us we could sit anywhere we wanted in the theater, but not the two rows near the middle. Those were reserved for Elvis and his specially invited guests. He told us everything at the concession stand was free, and that we could go as much as we liked. We were told the only time the concessions were off limits was when Elvis went to the stand. On those occasions, everyone was supposed to stay in their seats until he returned to his. These simple rules seemed easy to follow, and it wouldn't be long before I found out the reason for them.

I remember the first time I was ever invited to the private show, and it makes me sigh. The memories are still fresh in my mind, even after all these years, and they still rouse a place in my heart. As I hold the diary in my hands, a part of me wants to just put it back in the bag and return it the shelf. Just leave it alone. I thought, this was all far from your mind before you stumbled across it. But I know this is a battle I cannot win. Like those of us struggling with our weight, the temptation of the candy in the pantry is great. It matters not if it is right in front, or hidden on the top shelf, the enticement for it can be overwhelming. Before I can think of one good reason not to, the diary is open to the entry…

Dec. 27 1969

…Messed around the house all day. Terry and I were going to show, but it started too early, so I said let's go by Elvis' house. We got in and played in the yard and hung around the guard shack. Then, after about two hours, we went with Elvis and the others to the movies. Elvis kept turning around looking at me and winking. He finally sent Charlie back to me and said Elvis wants you to go meet him up front. I couldn't believe it. I went up to the balcony steps and sat at the bottom. Elvis came back there and said he wondered if I was Kathy from the summer. He couldn't figure out for sure. He said he didn't think he would ever see me again. He sat by me a long time and kept his hand on my leg. He was so good, he rubbed my legs and up my shirt on my back. Then we went back to the show. Afterwards, Terry and I left for home and went to bed…

I remember how hard it was to sleep that night. I pinched myself more than once to see if it was all a dream. It had to be, because I just couldn't believe Elvis would even have the slightest interest in me. I was shy and quiet, nothing like the glamorous people he always seemed to be surrounded by. I was not homely as a teenager, but certainly nothing like the beautiful starlets he shared the screen with in his Hollywood movies. I convinced myself if it was just a dream, I did not want it to end. Besides, I thought dreams only lasted one night, and Elvis had begged me to come to the movie the following evening. It was an invitation I could not refuse.

Dec. 29, 1969

…Worked. Came home and got ready to go to Elvis' house. Sat around the guard house about one hour, then went to the show. Elvis told Charlie to let me sit by him so Terry and I sat on his row. Everyone kept staring at us wondering who we were! I went to the bathroom and before I got back Elvis had come to the front. He was waiting on me coming out of the bathroom. He put his arm around me so tight. I could feel everything. He held me so close and breathed so heavy in my ear. He kept kissing all over my neck and face. He whispered in my ear he needs my number at work and home so he could reach me. He said he remembered me for sure now from the summer. We made out and he kept turning around looking in the back, then he would kiss me good. Then we went back to the show. Stayed till about 4:00 a.m. Went to bed…

That was the second time he had asked for my

number, but this time I knew he was really serious about it. Because unlike the last time he had asked for it, this time he had given me his. In the back of my diary, written on the inside of the worn cover, it reads;

Elvis' house number- 397-4427.

Reading the number once again, I am tempted to pick up the phone and dial it. I wonder who would answer, and if they had any idea who the number used to belong to. If I did dial it, I could only be disappointed by whoever answered, for there would be no comparison to the sound of his voice. His "Hello" is something that once stirred my heart and a memory I shall never forget.

Whatever hopes I had of just closing the diary and putting it away are now hopelessly gone. The book and its contents seem to pulse in my hand. I am resigned to the fact that what I have started, I must see through to the end. With every turn of the page, there is an endless parade of memories. Memories as strong as any flood and just as hard to contain. Although this all transpired a long time ago, for me, it feels like only yesterday. I suppose that is the way it shall always be. But if a person must go through all of eternity with only their memories, what wonderful ones I shall have.

I carefully turn the page to the next entry and something slips from between the pages onto the floor. It is the empty cellophane bag from some Hershey's Kisses. As I hold the well preserved bag in my hand, I remember how Elvis had selected them especially for me. He had gone behind the counter of the concession stand to get them and presented them to me along with a real kiss. Like the cellophane wrapper, the time and place are noted forever on the page, and the memories are as sweet as the candy that once filled it.

Dec. 30, 1969

...Worked. Got ready to go to the show with Elvis. We just went over to the show and waited on him. I went to the concession stand during the movie. Elvis followed me and went behind the counter and picked some Hershey's Kisses for me. Then he kissed me real good. He asked me while I was up there if I was leaving. I asked him if he was going to watch another show and he said he was but he'd rather make a show with me in the bathroom. He grabbed my hand and started to the side of the stand. We went into the men's bathroom and he kissed me all over. He said he could hardly stand to look at me without kissing me. There was a couch in the bathroom and we laid on it and made out for about 30 minutes. Then I said I better go back and check on Terry. He said he would see me soon. We watched another show and he went back every time I went. We had fun. He always tries to feel me when he kisses me. I can't believe his hand was in my blouse. He whispers in my ear and says

*he is crazy over me. Went home around 3:00
and went to bed...*

When I finished reading that entry, I am
reminded of all the times we came home so early
in the morning. I suppose by now many of you are
wondering what my parents were doing while all
of this was going on. Daddy was tired from
working all day and usually in bed by 10:00. As
for mother, she was filled with trust, and it made
me feel bad to sneak around behind her back. I
knew this was something they would never have
approved of, but I desperately didn't want it to
end. I was living a dream--something I would
have never thought possible. Extraordinary
encounters like this do not happen to ordinary
girls like me. Those events are reserved for
children's fairy tales, not something that could
ever possibly come true. And yet, here it was
happening to me, just plain old Kathy. So I ask
you not judge me, or mother and daddy too
harshly, but only try to understand what an
unbelievably magical time this was to a 16 year-
old girl.

Over time, mother became ever more
suspicious, and the late hours I had been keeping
were beginning to make us fight. If the friction
between us wasn't enough, Christmas break was
over, and it was time to go back to school. What a
report I could have given about how I had spent
my break, but it was something I couldn't share. I
suppose my time with Elvis had its price, and the
cost would be my high school years. In school, I

was just plain Kathy, and oh how I would have liked to have showed up the popular girls. But I knew I could not tell a soul, or else they would want to go with me and prove it. I didn't want to take a chance that Elvis would become upset and end it, so I kept the secret. It was a hard thing to do. I suppose it was like Lois Lane knowing who Superman was and not being able to tell anyone. It was a price I gladly paid.

As a parent, a mother's trust can only go so far, and it wasn't much longer before it became even more strained between us. Like the movie theater, Elvis had another place he liked to go just to get away. I don't know when he started going there, but he used to keep a couple of rooms at the Howard Johnson's Motor Lodge. It was down the street from Graceland, and Terry and I went there with him for parties many times. He always had two rooms that adjoined, and there was always plenty of sandwiches and soda. The men that followed him like a shadow were always there, but Elvis spent plenty of time alone in the other room with me.

Just like my first invitation to the private movie show, I can clearly remember the day Charlie called to invite us to a party. It was something that happened quite frequently, and Terry and I were asked to go many times. Sometimes we would go there after the movies, and on others, we just went straight to the motel. Charlie always wanted us to park around in back so as not to attract attention. I smile when I think how the "Vomit Comet" must have looked next to the Cadillacs out back. I turn to the page which recalls the first time we ever went, and yet another wave of emotions washes over my heart. I read to you now what is written in the handwriting of an excited teenager, a long time ago.

Jan. 5, 1970

…Charlie called and said Elvis wanted us to come over to Howard Johnson's and have a party. We got ready and went. We waited for Elvis for about 30 minutes. He came and sat by me on the bed the whole time. He kept looking at me and kissing me. He sang me about three songs during the whole night and he looked into my eyes while he sang. He had a drink of grapefruit juice and vodka. He told me to taste it and see if I liked it. I took a sip and it was terrible. He got on to me because he said I didn't even get a good taste. He pulled up my vest and rubbed my stomach while we were sitting on the bed. He scratched my back and I scratched his practically all night. He was rubbing my hand and started kissing it. Then he looked at my hands for a long time. I pulled them away and hid them behind my back because they looked terrible. He kept pulling them back and telling me, "I am very observant, and your hands are not boney, and they remind me very much of my mother's". I felt a little better…

The news came on the radio and he squatted down in front of the radio on the floor. Then he looked at me and held out his arm for me to come and sit by him. I squatted down between his legs and he held me so close to him I could hardly breathe. He kept squeezing me and kissing the top of my head. Then we lay down on the floor facing each other. He was on his back and I had one arm across his stomach leaning over him. He kept looking at me not smiling or saying anything. Then he would laugh and kiss me. I thought he would never quit. I was trying to straighten my hair and he fixed it for me. He flattened it all over and laughed. I straightened his for him and brushed his hair from his forehead. He said he wondered if he would ever see me again after last summer and then he kissed me gently on my forehead. He looked me in the eyes and said. "I believe if a person really concentrates and thinks hard about someone, then that person thinks about him at the same time."

Then Terry came into the room and said we had better be going. He said, "Damn. I sure hope I can be alone with you sometime," and then he said "Maybe someday we will." I went into the other room and got my coat to leave. Then he put both arms around my neck and put my coat around me. Then he laid his forehead against mine and we just looked at each other. He kissed me and held me close. Finally Terry said "I hate to say this, but Kathy has to go to school tomorrow". Then he asked her if I couldn't just stay home from school. He said "Boy, when you start aching all over that's pretty bad." He kissed me again for a long time and whispered in my ear…

Photo Album

The house my Daddy built by hand in 1952. It has stood the test of time and remains to this day on Homewood Rd. in Memphis.

My sisters and I with Daddy in the pool he dug by hand. 1960

LEFT: Terry (standing), Kathy, and Karen at Christmas. 1959

BELOW: Pony Daddy got us for Christmas in 1960. Terry (10), Kathy (7), Karen (3)

Thanksgiving 1969

Terry and Kathy on the motorcycle Redd bought
for them in 1970

Kathy (17) Graduation picture 1970

The playhouse my Daddy built for me with real linoleum floors. It was my sanctuary; a place when I was young that never harbored anything except dreams and love.

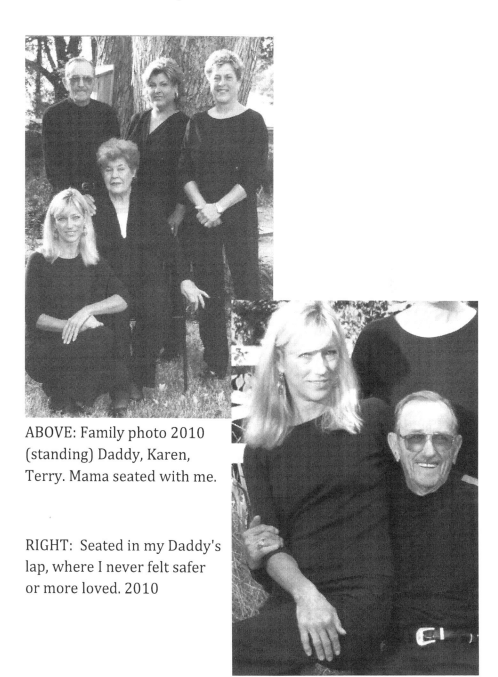

ABOVE: Family photo 2010
(standing) Daddy, Karen,
Terry. Mama seated with me.

RIGHT: Seated in my Daddy's
lap, where I never felt safer
or more loved. 2010

July 3rd, 1969. Taken at Graceland the night Elvis placed the Love Beads gently around my neck.

July 3rd, 1969. After he gave me the beads I asked him to let me take his picture. In the years we were together; this photo was the only thing I ever asked from him.

7

"I WANT YOU TO COME TO VEGAS WITH ME."
It was something I never thought he would say to
me. I was shocked, for this was too marvelous and
amazing to believe. I could think of nothing else
as my pen put down the words in my diary. I
dreamed of being backstage at one of his events,
watching the crowds of people as they pushed and
strained for his attention. I imagined peeking
through the silk curtains as the spotlight shown
upon him, and I vividly imagined the women
swoon as he came nearer to them. Oh, what a
grand dream that was, but as is usually the case, it
would not be so.

I closed the diary for a moment and recalled
the frustration that invitation had brought into my
life. Of course mother had said no when I asked
her. No amount of persuasion could change her
mind. I was so angry with her. Here was a chance
of a lifetime for me, and the only thing that stood
in the way of my dreams was my mother. She
couldn't understand why Elvis would want me to
go with him, and there was no way I could tell

her. Oh, how tempted I was to just blurt it out, but I knew if I did it would all come to an end. That was something I just didn't want to happen. After awhile, I became resigned to the fact that I would not be going, but the feelings of anger toward my mother lingered for a long time. Even after all these years, I can still imagine how grand that trip would have been. Only with hindsight can I now see the wisdom in my mother's decision.

Thinking about that time again, I remembered the conversation I had with my daughter Brittney just the other day. She was at odds with how to deal with my 14 year-old granddaughter Timeri and her desire to have a little more freedom. Like most mothers, she wasn't as worried about her as she was with the girls she might be hanging around with. Not that they were bad or anything, only that the times are so much different. It seems like our kids are bombarded with so much information, and unfortunately for them, most of it they are not ready for. They also seem to lack supervision, with many parents detached from their children's lives. For many of these young adults, their homes and their schools have failed them. I am sad for the future of this country, for it looks very bleak to me.

I spoke that day with Brittney about the dangers of putting too much pressure on Timeri. Like sitting on the top rail of a fence, she needed to find the perfect balance between a child's budding independence and a mother's strong need to guide. While I could sympathize with her dilemma, I had no real answers for her. This was something she would have to figure out for herself; I had every confidence she would find the right path. Life has a way of nudging us in the direction we need to go. Sometimes it seems like that path is the hardest and has the most obstacles, but with time, we all seem to end up where we were meant to be.

Children are so much older for their age than when I was growing up, and they are much more knowledgeable of the ways of the world. Still they are but children, and there is much danger hidden in the glare of becoming an adult. Like all of us, from the time we first clomped around in our mother's shoes, we have longed to be women. Wearing our mother's old dress, a necklace of beads around our neck, a purse draped across our arm, only seemed to reinforce our wish. We so wanted to be grown and thought we would bust while we waited for it to happen. Only as adults do we understand the concept of time. Perhaps with advancing age we understand it even more, for it now seems to speed by like the wind. How fun it would be to clomp around once again in childlike innocence, but like my days with Elvis, that time only lives in my memories.

With thoughts of my anger with mother fading from my mind, my attention is drawn back to the diary resting in my hand. With a sigh, I remember the trip never taken and turn the page.

Jan. 6, 1970

…Charlie called and wanted us to meet at the movie. He said we needed to park around

behind the movie so lots of people won't be getting in. We were almost the first ones to get there. Terry and I sat down on the row right behind Elvis' seat and as soon as he walked in, he leaned over his seat and kissed me. He said he thought he couldn't keep from going crazy until he saw me again. About halfway through the movie I went to the bathroom and when I got up Elvis got up too and walked up the other aisle. We got up front and he grabbed my hand and put me up against the wall and kissed me really hard and long. (He feels great) I told him mother had said I couldn't go to Vegas, and as he wiped a tear from my eye he said, "Maybe next time." He told me not to be too upset with her and said mothers usually know what's best. Then we went to the couch in the men's bathroom. He said he would close the movie soon if I could go to the house and stay awhile. Terry said okay, so after about 45 minutes we left. We went up the back drive and parked. Charlie and Terry went to watch TV downstairs; I went to watch TV with Elvis in another room. We ate some peanut butter sandwiches and milk. We lay on the floor with pillows all night and he kept tickling me. I'd tickle him back, but he wouldn't let me breathe when I started laughing. Then he would hold his mouth over mine and kiss me forever. (Really good) Then he got on top of me and really started going crazy. I was afraid Charlie would walk in, but he didn't. Elvis said I need to think about him every night at 10:00 really hard and he'll think of me. We went to the den and he said Terry needed to let me stay the night. Terry said mother would be getting mad, so we went home and went to bed...

I closed the diary and remembered that long winter of 1970. It was perhaps the most melancholy time of my life, made worse after Elvis went to Las Vegas without me. I was so upset with mother for not letting me go, and I blamed her for the reason we were not together. I worried most every day that he would find someone else to replace me, and that perhaps I might never see him again. I was never more confused about my feelings for Elvis, and the outcome of our affair, than I was at that period of my life. At times it was overwhelming, and I wished I did not have to go through it by myself. Perhaps if I could have had someone to share it all with, it might have been a little easier. But I guess that is the nature of secrets, and the loneliness their knowledge sometimes brings.

I was naïve at 16, but I wasn't stupid. I knew he was married and that being with him was wrong. Still, I could not help the way I felt about him. To be in his embrace once again consumed my dreams, and my every waking thought seemed to revolve around him. I guess in my mind, I justified the affair by telling myself he was the one who was cheating. After all, he was the one who was married. Still, I worried about being caught by Priscilla, and I thought I would die if that ever happened. I worried about the confrontation that would occur, but mostly I feared she would put a final end to it. I hoped it could remain a secret, at least until Elvis decided to alter their relationship. It was something he had talked about more than once with me.

I now know how that would all work out, but at the time I had my dreams of a future with him. I knew he was about to have his 35th birthday that January, and I really didn't care about the difference in our ages. After all, daddy was ten years older than mother, and I was practically 17. It was a birthday I celebrated without him, for it happened while he was in Vegas. The diary only speaks briefly about the occasion, and the tone of the entry is quite bland. As I skim through the entries, I find my life while he was gone had returned to the boring and the monotonous. There are only a couple of entries about him, and they only speak of the telegram Terry and I had sent to him wishing him good luck. He didn't reply, so we assumed he hadn't received it. I hoped that was all it was, but I couldn't help thinking that he really had found someone else.

I carefully turn page after page, and my life progresses without a single mention of Elvis in the entries. There are many about school and work, and the babysitting I did, but none written with the slightest glow. They are as dull as the days they describe. The only events worth mentioning were sorority dances I went to with

Terry at Memphis State. She was very involved in everything at school, and as I mentioned before, conversation came easy to her. She had many friends she hung around with--most of them were either on the football team or played basketball. One of her friends was Larry Finch, and if you know anything at all about Memphis basketball, you know who he was. All I remember about him was how much he smiled, and how much he loved to play cards. He was the one who taught her how to play spades, and they played all the time between classes.

At one of the dances she took me to, I ran into Michael--a boy I hadn't seen since elementary school. We always hung around together when we were younger, and he was just the nicest boy. He was as sweet as he was good looking, and I sometimes wish I had shown him the slightest interest. We danced a few times together, but there was no spark between us. What chance did any boy in high school have when the bar was set so high by Elvis? He was the polished diamond that shown with such brilliance. Perhaps I didn't look deep enough into Michael's heart to see the diamond still obscured by the coal. In life, we all have regrets, and he is one of mine. He was a real keeper, and it sometimes bothers me that I never even gave him a chance. Oh well, just a little too much water has passed under that bridge.

I skim through the pages that pass from winter to spring, remembering the small events that made their way into the diary. Then, as if the sun had burst through the clouds, I read...

June 2 1970

…Worked 9 to 5. Came home and went shopping. Charlie called and said Elvis is coming home Friday. Too excited to sleep but went to bed…

Seemed like everything got a little brighter after that entry. Memories I haven't thought about in years seemed fresh once again. I remembered how excited I was when I heard he was coming back home. I also remember how disappointing it was, because we were leaving on a two-week vacation to Florida before he got back. We had a great time on that trip, but it is still the only vacation I can remember when I couldn't wait for it to be over. I knew Elvis was home and couldn't wait to see him. Still, in the back of my mind I wondered if he would be as anxious to see me. My plan was to return home, play it cool, and wait until I heard from him. As it turned out, I didn't have to wait very long.

June 22, 1970

…Messed around all day. Worked in the yard. Charlie called and we went to the show with Elvis. At the movies Elvis came to the refreshment stand and grabbed my hand. He pulled me close and sang "You've lost that loving feeling" into my ear and squeezed me tight on my back. After the show Charlie begged us to come to the house so we did. Everybody was at the gate when we got

there. Richard Davis drove up after we parked our car and said get in. Everyone just stared. They couldn't believe it. We parked by all of Elvis' other cars, then went in the back where Richard lives. We sat around and in a few minutes Charlie came over and we talked for awhile. Charlie likes me a lot better now and he kept calling me "Pretty Face" and "Smiling Eyes." He knows that is what Elvis calls me. Elvis was in the room with the slot cars with the rest of the boys. We had to leave soon. They didn't want us to leave and said we would have to come back when we could stay longer. We left and when Charlie drove us back down everyone was still there staring at us. Came home and went to bed...

As I recall, there were quite a few nights when I was with Elvis that nothing much happened. Don't get me wrong, I loved every minute that I spent with him, but sometimes it seemed like the boys came first. It might be a game of tackle football in the yard, or sometimes it was something stupid and dangerous. I remember one cold evening around Christmas time, hiding for my life in the nativity scene. Elvis and the boys were chasing each other around lighting fireworks and throwing them at each other. I was scared to death, but to them, this was something they thought was fun.

Sometimes their activities bordered on the macabre. On more than one occasion, after the movies were over, he would want to go to the funeral home and look at bodies. This was something I had no desire to do, and quite frankly don't know why anyone would. I think the funeral parlor was somewhere behind the house, and I remember him telling Terry and me he had permission to go there. Apparently it was something he and the boys liked to do, but it was something I never talked about with him. It was a side of him I found easy to block out, and I wondered how much effect this gang of men had over his life.

There were other things about being with Elvis that made me uncomfortable. For starters, he was so bold sometimes and would kiss me passionately in front of people I didn't know. I constantly worried about being seen by someone, but it was hardly something he gave a second thought. For the most part, these were his people and friends, and I suppose he had no fear around them. It did little to put me at ease, and I constantly worried we would be caught.

The uncomfortable feeling was never worse than when Priscilla was at the movies with us. She usually had a couple of girlfriends that sat next to her, and sometimes Elvis would have me sit right behind her. He would constantly turn around smiling and winking at me. I would about die when he would pretend to stretch and would squeeze and rub my leg behind her back. I would grab his hand to stop, but that only seemed to make him want to do it more. Sometimes he even followed me to the concession stand and would kiss me passionately in the lobby. It was a strange mix of fear and excitement every time I was with him, and over time it was just something I tried to get used to.

As I hold the diary in my hands and remember those meetings so long ago, I wonder if she knew. I suppose she did, but I never spoke a single word to her. She wasn't much older than me, and it's possible she was just as naive as I was. Still, I find it hard to believe that she didn't. Maybe it was something she had just gotten used to, or maybe she just didn't care. As I said before, I never talked to her, so I'll not put words or feelings into her mouth. I will take the time to tell her how sorry I am and hope she can forgive the actions of an infatuated teenage girl. I know being young is not an excuse for what I did, but maybe, more than anyone else, she can remember how it was to be with him. I hope so, for it was never my intention to harm anyone. I am truly sorry.

As I wipe a tear that has trailed down my cheek, the evening has grown late, and my husband Phil has long since turned in for the night. I hesitate to open the diary once again, but it has become nearly impossible to put down. I open to the entries describing a hot steamy summer, one that still makes my heart skip a beat. It has been quite awhile since those days long ago, and yet, there are so many memories…

AS I SIT HERE NOW IN THE STILLNESS
of the evening, I can hear the crickets as they
chirp their nightly chorus outside my window.
While I listen to the rhythmic sounds, the question
I have asked myself a thousand times pops into
my head. Why me? Of all the women who were
lined against the gates of Graceland the night we
first met, why had Elvis chosen me? He had
kissed many girls as he worked his way around
the gate, and yet, I was the one he had invited in. I
suppose it's a question I will never have an
answer to. At the time, it was something I never
really gave much thought. Only as I read the diary
entries do the questions return, and, as always, I
have no answer. I only know that he did--I guess
that will just have to do.

With only the light from my small nightstand
to read by, I slide under the covers of my bed.
With my pillow propped against the headboard, I
lean back and once again open the diary.

July 1, 1970

… Charlie called and said we need to meet at the movie tonight. We got there early before anyone else and sat right behind Elvis' seat. Elvis came to sit down and leaned over the aisle and kissed me really good. Elvis kept smiling and looking at me all night. He said I made him crazy all the time. Every time I'd go up front Elvis would go and we would make out for a long time. He really likes me. Charlie took me to the balcony one time and tried to fool around. I just said no and went back downstairs. If Elvis knew what he did, he would really be mad. I never said anything to him about it. I told Elvis we had to go before the movie was over, and he said he had to tell me good-bye first. We went to the front and he kissed me hard and squeezed me against him tight! (I could feel everything) He would breathe hard on my neck and say I couldn't leave him yet. I told him I had to or I'd be in trouble. Went home and went to bed…

After reading about that night at the movies, it brought forth many vivid memories. The first was Charlie and his attempt to lure me into the balcony. I don't know if he had been drinking or not, but I suspect he had. It was very uncharacteristic of him, and something he never tried again. We were friends, but nothing more, and after that night at the movie I think he knew it. When it came to Elvis, I really don't know what

we were or where we were going. I never started
out thinking anything was ever going to come of
it. In fact, in the beginning it surprised me every
time I was ever with him. I always thought one
day I would just never hear from him again, and it
would all just end. One day it would, but not for
the reasons you may think. Before I can get to that
day, there would be many more secret nights
between us.

July 4, 1970

*...Stayed around the house all day. Charlie
called and said he would call back later
about what we were doing that night. When
he called again, he said not to tell anyone we
were going to go to the back door instead of
the front. We did and Richard came and let us
in. They had saved us a seat right behind
Elvis. When I walked in and sat down, he
said, "Hi love." All during the show he would
turn around and look at me. Once he was
yawning and he just patted my face while he
had his arms stretched behind him. Then he
said, "Hey Kathy, come here." I leaned
forward and he kissed me. This was the
second time. Then he whispered in my ear
that he wanted Terry and me to go to the
Howard Johnson's after the show was over. I
told him I didn't think we could because we
had to be home by 2:30. He said, "If you'll
go, then we won't show any more movies and
leave." I said okay. Show was over and we*

walked out with him. He walked me to the car and spun me around and leaned me against the door and kissed me hard. Then he started kissing me like he was going mad and pressed himself hard against my legs. Then he said to follow him and Charlie. They went extra slow so we could keep up with them. We passed them once and he looked out the window and puckered his lips like he wanted a kiss. We were the first ones at the motel and we parked next to them and went in. I sat on the bed and he lay down next to me and pulled me close to him. I laid my head against his chest and he started kissing me. He wouldn't quit for nothing. Then he rolled me over and got on top of me. We stayed like that awhile, then he started kissing me real fast and was laughing and tickling me. I was about to die for some air. Then he sat up on me and I was just laying there looking at him and he would lean over and kiss me again. While we were kissing Terry came into the room to check on me and Elvis told her she could trust him. Then he started tickling me again. Then we lay next to each other for awhile and he put his arm under my neck and we watched TV for awhile. He turned me towards him and I looked him deep in his eyes. I pushed his hair away from his face and ran my fingers through it. Then he cupped my face in his hands and kissed me on the side of my neck. While we were kissing he just reached down and unsnapped his belt and threw it on the floor. Later I got up and tried it on. It was all great. Everyone else was in the other room the whole time having a party. Finally Terry said we had to go. He asked me why and I said because mother told us we had to be home by 2:30. He just kept kissing me and I got up and he put his arm around me and walked me to the door. I kept trying to pull away but he kept pulling me back. While he was kissing me goodnight he was squeezing my butt tight against him with his hands. I turned around while I was walking to the car and he was leaning against the door looking at me. He stood there until we drove off...

Once when we were kissing, he looked up and told Terry he was going to end up making a sex maniac out of me. Then he added, "Or she's going to make one out of me". While I was on my back, he was patting out a tune on my stomach and softly sang a song in my ear. Went to bed...

I carefully refold the two sheets of paper that entry was written on and put it back in its place in the diary. This space between the pages has been its home for many years, but it doesn't seem that long ago that I wrote it. I remember how tired I used to be when I would get home, and of how hard I tried to remember every detail of what had happened that night. While the spelling and punctuation weren't always correct, I always did my best to remember every detail before I went to bed. No matter how late or how tired I was, this was just something I had to do before I could sleep. If I even could.

Why did I feel the need to put it on paper? I honestly don't know. I guess it was all so fantastic to me at the time, I just had to. I guess if I had to have a reason, it was because I just wanted some kind of proof. I knew even then I would one day tell someone, but I never thought it would be like this. Perhaps it is better this way, for if my children and grandchildren must learn about my affair with Elvis, I would much rather they hear it from me. I hope they will understand how overwhelming it all was for me. I am not proud of what happened between us, but I was just as powerless to stop it. When Elvis wanted to see me, I went. I could not tell him no. The diary entries are proof of that, and so they have served their purpose.

I adjust my pillow and open the diary once again. On the adjoining page another heavily creased piece of paper slides from its place in my history. After carefully unfolding it, I anxiously await what is written on the faded lines. Like stepping back in time and place, I relive the entry…

July 6, 1970

…Charlie called to see if we could come to the house tonight. We got there about 11:00 and there were people all around the gate. We drove to the gate and everyone stared at us as we drove up to the house. When we got there Charlie and Richard came outside to

*show us where to go in. We stayed in the
back den all night. I can't believe we were
about the only people there. Elvis got there
after a few minutes. We ate ham sandwiches,
chips, and snacks all night and watched TV.
Elvis had on a beautiful gold family tree. I
told him I liked it. He said one day I could
wear it or have one like it if I would just be
patient. I'm sure! He also had on his gold
and diamond bracelet. I love it. He let me try
it on and I wore it all night for him. He said,
"Kathy, you have the most beautiful eyes
I've ever seen," and then he called me
"Laughing Eyes" again. We went to a couch
in the corner and made out all night. He
didn't care who was watching us. He told me
to give him all of my attention and quit
worrying about everyone looking. It made
me nervous. He really wanted to be by
ourselves and I couldn't believe all he did. I
unbuttoned his shirt and ran my hands over
his tanned chest. Then he just took it off and
said I'd be more comfortable if I took mine
off too. He started unbuttoning my blouse
and I grabbed his hand and said, "You're
crazy--not in front of all these people." He
laughed and said, "I'll just do like this." and
put his hands under my blouse. He asked me
if I'd like to be with him all the time. I said
yes and he said I'd probably wear him out. I
asked him what about Priscilla, and he said
she wouldn't always be around to worry
about. We stayed by ourselves in the corner*

*all night and he begged me to stay longer but
I told him I had to get home because it was
nearly 5:00 a.m. We had a great night. Went
home and went to bed...*

As I finished reading the entry, I tried to
recall what I was feeling when I wrote it. I
remember wondering if he was serious when he
said things about Priscilla, and if I might really
have a future by his side. I was captivated by him,
of that there can be no doubt. But was I in love
with him? It's hard for me to describe exactly
how I felt, because the whole situation just
seemed so impossible. He was a married man and
was arguably the most famous person in the
world. I was just plain Kathy--at school and at
home--yet he wanted to be with me. He asked me
many times while we were together if I could be
patient. I told myself then if Elvis wanted me to
wait for him, I would wait as long as it took. It
wasn't long before the way I truly felt about him
found its way into my journal.

July 8, 1970

*...Charlie called today and said Elvis
wanted us to meet him at the house tonight.
We got ready and left about 10:00. We all
had fun tonight. Elvis and I stayed in our
room most of the night and talked. He is so
sweet and I love for him to hold me close. He
puts both of his hands on my face when he
kisses me and I love how tender he is. He
really wants us to try to go to Vegas with*

him next time they go. I told him maybe he could talk mama into letting us go. He said maybe he'd try to think up something good to tell her. He looked so good tonight. He had on gray pants and a royal blue shirt. He had on a big wide white belt. We watched a good happy movie on TV and ate some snacks. I hope we get to be together again soon. I think I really love him. We stayed until about 4:00 and then I had to get home. Got home and went to bed...

There it was--in bold writing near the end of the entry. I was in love with him. I suppose in some obscure way I am still am. I've often heard you never really forget your first love, and while I don't often think about him, I guess I never really did. The early entries in this journal are scattered with fledgling feelings of love, but that's all they ever were. When it came to Elvis, he was my first true love. Right or wrong, my feelings for him could no longer be denied. We talked more than we ever had that night, and most of it was about the future. He told me, once again, he would soon be leaving, but I can't remember if it was to Vegas or California. I guess it really didn't matter since I knew I wouldn't be going with him. Mama was never going to let that happen. We still had some time before he had to leave, and we were together once again.

July 10, 1970

...Elvis called today around 3:00 and said we were going to the movies tonight. We got there around 11:00 and there were lots of people Charlie wouldn't let in. We got some Milk Duds and a coke, then went to sit down. Elvis was sitting down and turned around and told me to come and sit next to him. Terry sat with Charlie. We kissed and made out all night. We went to the front a few times together and stayed for about an hour or more. I tried his shoes on up front and walked around in them. He thought I looked so funny. We went back inside and watched all the movies. He held me so close all through the movies and kept his hands all over me. Came home and went to bed. It was around 5:00 a.m.

I can still remember how it felt to be in his embrace. The touch of his hands, the smell of his cologne, the feel of his kiss--all these things and more are forever ingrained in my memory. I wanted to be with him all the time and hated always having to meet like this. At times, it seemed as if we were all alone in the darkened theatre, but I always knew we were not. It made me so nervous when we were around other people; I constantly thought someone would say something to Priscilla. I did not want it to end like that. Thankfully that day never came, or if it did I never heard about it. We kept on with our secret romance, and as I turn to the next entry I see we were not apart for long.

July 11, 1970

...Elvis had Charlie call and wanted to see if we could go to Howard Johnson's tonight. We got there and Charlie took Terry to one room to get stuff out to eat. Elvis met me at the car when we drove up and said he was afraid we weren't going to get to come. I told him I had to see him and he said, "I'm so afraid I'm going to lose you! I'm going crazy!" We went to our room while everyone else stayed next door at the party. We sat on the bed awhile and then decided to lie down--we stayed there for hours. Terry came over two or three times and knocked on the door and Elvis would say "Kathy is OK. I'm taking good care of her." Then he would kiss me forever! I thought sometimes I couldn't breathe when he was on top of me. After a long time we went next door to get something to eat. I sat on the corner of the bed and Elvis fixed his plate and sat down beside me. He kept whispering in my ear to hurry and eat so we could go have dessert in our room. We watched TV with all the people for a long time. Terry kept saying we didn't have long and we needed to go home soon. We went to our room for a good while and just lay in the bed. He just kept kissing me and running his hands all over my body. He said this was wonderful and he'd never let me go home. I told him I didn't have time and we needed to stop before we went too far. He asked me to beg mother to let me go

with him to Vegas! I hope mama will let us go. He said he would take good care of me all the time! Terry finally came to our room and said we had to get home before we got in trouble. We left and he said he would call tomorrow. Went home and I could hardly sleep all night...

I refolded the slip of paper and returned it to the diary, with memories of those days flooding my heart. But along with the good were the bad. I remembered the constant and pressing friction with mother, the cost of my secret affair. I remember how much I begged her to let Terry and me go with Elvis to Vegas. It was all in vain, for mother wasn't listening to any of it. She just couldn't understand why he would want to take us, and it was a hopeless feeling for me knowing I couldn't tell her.

As I lie here in my bed in the quiet of the night, I wonder what would have happened if I had just blurted it all out. Mother would have been shocked; as I'm sure she will be when she reads about the secrets once hidden in my diary. But that was a long time ago, in what now seems like another life, and to return to that time I need only to turn the page...

9

꒰ꝏ꒱ꝏ꒱ꝏ꒱

WHILE MY HUSBAND SLEEPS PEACEFULLY next to me, I listen to his rhythmic breathing and open the diary. After reading a couple of rather ordinary entries, another folded piece of paper slips from between the pages. After carefully unfolding it, I read the entry…

July 15, 1970

…Charlie called and said they were going to the movies again tonight and could we go. Mama said we couldn't stay late, but we could go. I'm tired of mama getting mad. We went early to the show. When we got there we had to wait outside about ten minutes for Charlie to unlock the doors. Charlie said Elvis wanted me to walk to the back and see him before the movie started. I walked down the side aisle and could see Elvis standing in the back. He kept acting like he was throwing me kisses while I was walking towards him. When I got to him he said let's go sit back here on some steps. We really made out for a long time and he kissed me all over. He said I

was one teenage girl who really turned him on. We watched two movies together and Terry sat with Charlie behind us. Elvis asked Terry if we could go to the house again but she said she was afraid we would really make mama mad! After the show I walked outside in the back and Elvis put me up against his car and pushed himself up against me. He kissed me so long and hard. He said he would call me soon. Went home and went to bed...

With a sigh I closed the diary, and the battles waged with my mother played in my mind. I don't blame her, not in the least, for it was a long time ago. My mother did what she thought was right, like I would do if the same situation had cropped up with any of my children. Still, there were hard feelings between us, and the more I snuck off to be with Elvis, the worse it seemed to get. It got to the point where I couldn't wait to get out of her house. She was suspicious of everything I did and everywhere I went, and it is only in hindsight I see the worry I must have caused her. I am sorry, mother, but at the same time I am not. That time in my life was beyond compare, and I fear I would do it all over again if I had the chance. Still, it bothers me to have hidden it from you, and for that I am truly sorry.

Now with thoughts of a romance with Elvis, and arguments with mother fresh in my head, I know it will be impossible to sleep. I got up from the bed carefully so as not to disturb my husband, but it wasn't necessary. He is sleeping soundly as only a man can, and, as always, I am jealous of his ability to just let the day go. As for me, I will worry over the smallest things. They will consume my thoughts and keep me from the deep embrace of sleep--the sleep my husband now enjoys.

I am halfway to the kitchen before I realize the diary is still in my hands. I decide to make myself a nice cup of tea and read just a little more. It is quiet in the kitchen, with only the hum of the refrigerator breaking the stillness. It makes me recall the quiet in my room on the nights I wrote in this diary, and I take a seat at the table and open the book. It only takes a moment to find my place, and I am transported back in time to…

July 17, 1970

…Elvis called and wanted us to go to the movies tonight. We had a good time. Charlie likes Terry a lot I think. Elvis met me up front a lot and we kissed and made out a lot. Elvis got me some candy and a coke up front and gave it to me when I came out of the bathroom. We went to the men's room once and stayed a long time! Came home and went to bed…

That short entry was written on a scrap of paper torn from a notebook, written by a girl who was madly in love. How confusing it all was to me then, and yet, I'm still not sure it has become any clearer with the passage of time. I remember how that summer changed for me when Elvis left town, and it seemed like I spent most of my time crying. He was either in Vegas or California, and I was left behind to wonder if someone else would be taking my place. If his leaving wasn't bad enough, I was crushed when I found out Terry was moving to Atlanta.

While she was in college, she had started working part-time as a receptionist at a small business in town. One day, an executive with a major airline offered her a stewardess job. It was all so exciting for her, and after considering her options, she withdrew from school. Flight attendant school was in Atlanta and started in the fall. With her things all packed and the goodbyes all said, she left. I felt like I was losing my best friend, and I guess in a way I was. I knew, without Terry, there would never have been a relationship with Elvis. She was my cover, and with her by my side, it was harder for mother to say we couldn't go to meet him.

It wasn't as if we ever lied to her; we just never told her everything. Mother always assumed when we went to something with Elvis, we were part of a larger group of people. I guess she thought there were many kids going to his movies and parties, and we were only part of the crowd. I couldn't tell her the truth because that would mean the end of everything. I wasn't ready for that. The story of Cinderella was read many times to me as a child, and it was how I felt whenever Elvis and I were together. I didn't want the clock to strike midnight and return, once again, to the plain and ordinary girl who frequently showed up in my mirror.

There were many times when mother would make me cry when she said we couldn't go to see him, and it was all I could do to keep from just blurting it out. It almost happened later that summer. It was about two weeks before school started back, and we took a trip down to Destin. It was just mother, daddy, Karen, and me; it was probably the vacation I looked forward to the least. There wasn't much to do there, not like it is now, and I just wished it was already over. The car was packed full, and it seemed more like a move than a vacation.

Somewhere in Alabama, on what seemed like an endless stretch of two-lane highway, the car stalled out and we coasted to the side of the road. Daddy tried everything to get the car going again, but he needed a new part. Daddy and Karen started walking, while mother and I stayed in the car with all our stuff. They hadn't gone far before a nice man and woman stopped and gave them a lift to the next town. (People could be trusted back then.)

For a long time, mother and I didn't say much, but after awhile we began to talk. She surprised me when she apologized for our latest argument and told me of the biological change she was going through. She did her best to explain to me what she was experiencing, but at 17 it was hard for me to understand. (Believe me; I don't have that problem now.) It was the first time I can ever remember that mother and I had an adult talk, and it made me feel good. After we talked and laughed for a bit, she reached over and said, "How about some music?" and turned on the radio.

She turned the dial from side to side, trying to find a station that was not filled with static. She stopped on one that was fairly clear, and it was some kind of commercial. We kept talking, seeming to draw closer to each other with every passing moment. Then the announcer came back on said, "Here's one from Elvis," and mother said, "I just love his voice," and she turned up the volume. He was singing about a teddy bear--a song he used to softly sing into my ear, and it almost made me cry. I had to look away quickly from mother; it ripped at my heart that I couldn't be with him now. It was as close as I ever came to telling her everything, but instead I suggested we had better not run the battery down and turned the radio off. I don't remember talking much after that.

As I sit here in the quiet of my kitchen, the memories of my past swirl around my head like the smoke from a fire. So thick, it almost feels like I could brush them aside with my hand. Each one demands to be remembered and relived, and to have their turn played across the movie screen in my mind. It has been this way since I first found this diary, and their power and emotions will not be denied.

I have asked myself many times this night…Why? Why not just put this relic from my past back where I found it? Why go through this all over again? If you are waiting for some deep and mysterious reason, I'm afraid you will be disappointed. I guess if I have to give one, I will simply say this. At the age of 60, the ability to be 17 again, and in love with Elvis, all with only the turn of a page, is more than I can resist.

I now know for sure I will not sleep this night, so with a fresh cup of tea, I am determined to relive this diary until its conclusion. I open the tattered cover, and with a few turns of the pages I am returned to 1970. The entries are plain, almost mundane, and I skim from day to day looking for something exciting. I see at the end of August of that year, I started my senior year in school. There are lots of entries about work and babysitting, and occasional mentions of talking with Terry on the phone, but nothing from Elvis.

I flip through month after month of the same-- entries which seem as dry as a piece of toast. Occasionally there are entries about Terry, when she would come home for visits. As a flight attendant, she was able to fly for free and would sometimes come home for the weekends. It was always fun having her at home and it would be just like old times. She was still active in her sorority at Memphis State, so she would take me with her to parties and different functions. I never realized how much I missed her until it was time for her to leave again.

I guess this was a time in my life when I needed someone in it. Things were worse with mother, and I just seemed to drift through the days. As the holidays approached, it seemed like all I did was go to school and work or babysat.

Then one day, Aunt Ruby introduced me to a boy who worked in another department at Lowenstein's. He was a few years older than me, nearly 21, and Aunt Ruby had known his family for years. We began talking some at work and on breaks, and after awhile he asked me to the movies.

That day was fateful in my life--both bitter and sweet, and it was hardly mentioned at all in the entries. This young girl, not yet 18, was oblivious to the path her life had just taken. I wish now--while I feel as if I am peering over her shoulder as she writes--I could have warned her.

For me, reading this diary entry is like sitting on the top of a beautiful hillside. The grass is green and is as soft as cotton against my skin. The sky is the clearest blue; there are no clouds to hide the rays of the sun. In the valley I can see a small silvery train making its way towards a long wooden bridge--a bridge which spans a wide and deep jagged crevice. It is all so peaceful, until I notice the train barreling from the other direction on the same set of tracks. The trains are not aware of each other's presence, and I want to wave my arms and shout a warning to the small train of silver to stop--but the past cannot be changed--it can only be learned from and remembered.

Gary was tall, about 6 feet 8, and I guess at the time he could have passed for good looking. After that first movie date, he called me just about every night, and we talked all the time at work. He had been saving his money for awhile which he used for a down payment on a brand new Z28

Camaro. He would pick me up at the house and drive me around with him. I guess my world just looked a little brighter from the passenger seat of his car.

My senior winter formal was fast approaching, and I remember desperately wanting to go. It would be my last one, and I hoped more than anything that Gary would ask me. I had dropped plenty of hints, but they never seemed to register with him. You can imagine my surprise when he finally decided to ask me to the dance.

It didn't leave me much time to find a dress, but I didn't care about that. I was going, and that's all that mattered. I suppose I was just glad to have someone who was--What? Real? I guess that's the word I am looking for. I was in love with Elvis, but he could not come as my date. In my imagination, I guess I always dreamed one day he would, and we would dance in front of my classmates. He would take me into his arms, and we would spin beneath the rainbow of swirling lights, while everyone watched in amazement. Our secret love would be exposed for all to see, and I would no longer be just plain Kathy, I would be--dreaming. It was never going to happen.

At least with Gary, I had someone to go with. He surprised me with a dozen roses when he picked me up for the dance. It touched my heart when he gave them to me; it was the first time I had ever received flowers from a boy. They seemed more beautiful to me than they probably were; still, it was a sweet thing for him to do.

He was a perfect gentleman on that cold winter evening, as he held the car door open for me. Once at the formal, we danced to almost every song, and he brought me punch when we rested. When I got cold, he took off his jacket and draped it around me and held my chair when I sat down. When the dance was over, we had breakfast at the Waffle House, and when we returned to my house, he kissed me goodnight when he walked me to the front door. It was a perfect evening.

Thinking back on that night, I wonder if it really was, or if it was just the way I wanted it to be. That is the beauty of hindsight and its unmistakable clarity, when compared against what is happening in the present. Almost every entry after that night has something about him in it, and he seemed to be with me all the time. Mother and daddy seemed to be tired of him always being around, and on many nights we weren't allowed to go to dinner or movies. Mother just didn't like me being gone all the time, and as for daddy, I think he just knew he wasn't right for me. It is an ability all daddies seem to have when it comes to their little girls, and mine was no different. Still, I found reasons to keep on seeing him.

On almost every page in the month of February 1971, there is something written about him. We went riding around in his car, were at the movies, or were out eating somewhere. We talked on the phone almost every night, or he would just show up at the house and we would watch TV with mother and daddy. He seemed to genuinely have feelings for me, and we kissed more often than just good night. I tried to find reasons why mother and daddy were wrong about him; I felt more determined than ever to prove them wrong.

In life, it's funny how when things seem their clearest, that is when we have the hardest time seeing. It was no different for me when it came to Gary. I wanted him to be Mr. Right, and so he was. Our relationship continued despite my parents' objections, but everything I thought I wanted with Gary seemed to slide off the tracks when I read the small slip of note paper in the crease of the page.

March 4 1971

...Charlie called and said we were going to the movie tonight. We had a good time. We were with Charlie when he let people in through the back door and then went to go sit down. Elvis kept trying to get me to go up to the front. He finally came over to me at the water fountain and said, "I needed to see you bad!" He kissed me real good. Watched movie and then went home around 2:30 and went to bed. I know Elvis wants to be with me so bad. I love him to kiss me...

I had to stop reading when I came across that entry, and the turmoil my heart was going through played across my mind. Elvis had come back into my life, and I was more confused than ever. Now at the tender age of 18, my diary entries turned back to him, and the pages seemed to be a little brighter. And so, with the hum of the refrigerator in the background, and fresh memories in my head, I return to the diary and...

10

~~~~~

…ELVIS…

The entries following that night are filled with thoughts about Elvis, but yet Gary continued to occupy most of my time. We talked daily, either by phone or in person, but I could not bring myself to tell him about Elvis. What would I have said anyway? As I skim through the pages, I come to the entry dated…

March 9 1971

…Went to school and worked. Gary was there and he kept hugging on me and said something stupid that made me cry. Went home after work and Charlie called and wanted us to come to the party at the Howard Johnson's. Terry and I got to the motel about 11:00 and Charlie and Elvis were already inside with a few people. I didn't know what to say when we walked in so I just stood up against the end of the table and got a handful of chips. Elvis was talking to some people over by the window, but he

kept turning around and looking at me and smiling. Terry and I watched TV and Charlie was kissing all over Terry and I felt so stupid. I finally sat down on the corner of the bed and just watched everybody. Elvis came over in a little while and asked me if I was ready for him. I said I guess so. He sat on the bed behind me with his legs around the back of me. He sat right up against me and started blowing on the back of my neck. It felt great! Then he started kissing me on the cheek and softly sang part of a song into my ear. Terry came over and sat on the bed next to us for awhile. He kept telling her she needed to lose me one night and just leave me with him. I went to the bathroom and he fixed us a plate of food. He had a drink and told me I could share it with him. It tasted bad. I think it was bourbon and coke and I only drank a little every time. He said he really likes to talk to me and said he would always remember a blue-eyed blond girl from Memphis when he was old. Then he took me by the hands and kissed them and said we needed to go next door for a little while by ourselves. I got up and he took my arms behind me and said walk to the next room and I'll be right behind you. He was acting silly and laughing all the way in there. When we went into the room he changed the channel on the TV and we sat on the bed with pillows propped against the wall. He put his leg across mine and said, "I have you all to myself now and you're not getting away." Then he started kissing all over my neck. Then he started slipping his tongue into my ear and he was about to drive me crazy. He would breathe all over my chest and neck and it felt so good. Sometimes he would hum a tune into my ear, and then kiss me and smile. We made out really good and he went way too far and scared me. He promised he wouldn't do anything to get me in trouble. I don't think he would. After awhile we went to the other room and sat and talked to other people. Everyone laughed at all of Elvis' jokes. Even if they didn't like them, they acted like they did. We left about 3:30 and went home and went to bed. (I will always remember Room 48D.)

Closing the diary, I did indeed remember the room, and it seems like only yesterday I was there with him. I had been there many times with Elvis and the rest of his entourage, but this was the time I remember the most. What happened? I will tell you only this; it was a private moment between us, and I'll just leave it at that. Unlike now, women from my generation would never talk of such things, and that is the way it shall always remain with me. If you are looking for something that would cheapen the memory of Elvis, you will not find it in the pages of my diary, nor in the deepest recesses of my heart. It is a place he still resides in, even after all these years, and I hope this is something you can understand. So be it if you cannot.

The pull of the diary is strong, and it seems to demand that its contents be relived. It's funny that something from so long ago can have such an effect on me, but I'll not pretend that it doesn't. I quickly find my place and return to 1971.

There are more entries about Gary, and what can only be described as a very up and down few days. Some days I wrote about work, and of how Gary had been standoffish or moody, and then the next day he would hold my hand and kiss me. On the night of the following entry, we were supposed to have a date for that night. But at the last minute he made up an excuse, and it looked like I would be spending that night at home alone. That all changed when I read what happened next.

March 15 1971

...Was supposed to go out with Gary but he cancelled. He wasn't friendly and I came home after work. Charlie called and wanted to know if Terry and I could meet them at the Howard Johnson's. We got dressed and I wore my new sweater vest and knit pants. I like them a lot. We didn't get there until about 11:15, and everyone was sitting around watching TV and telling jokes. Elvis was talking to some of his friends and when he saw me come in he motioned for me to come and stand by him. He looked at me and said, "Hi Pretty Lips. I was wondering where you were." He introduced me to some

of his friends and said I was keeping him going, but tired! They all laughed but I was so embarrassed. We all talked for awhile, then I went over and sat at the foot of the bed to watch TV. Terry sat by me too and later Elvis came over and said, "Let's all get up here and get comfortable." We all sat up against the pillows and then Elvis said he needed a kiss from his "Pretty Lips" and he kissed me really long and hard. He said in my ear, "I hope I don't have to do without you too much." Then he took off his big wide belt and Terry got up and tried it on. She acted silly and Elvis loved it. He asked us if we were hungry and then fixed us a ham sandwich and coke. Charlie came in and asked Terry to come with him and meet some people, so she went into the other room. Elvis held my sandwich for me to take a bite. I didn't think I could swallow it because he kept watching me and then he would laugh. He stayed by me most of the night when we went into the other room. He didn't care if everyone saw him kiss me or have his hand on my leg. He even held my hand. Later he took me back to our room and he started kissing me all over. He acted like he was going crazy. I loved it but I was scared too! He told me again that he would never do anything to get me in trouble or hurt me. He wants me to just be patient for a little while longer and told me again that Priscilla wouldn't always be around. I told him finally we had better go because it was about 3:00 or so. We kissed and sat on the edge of the bed for awhile. Then he said he wanted me all night soon. Went home and went to bed. P.S. I know Elvis really loves me a lot. Room 48D

Then after a few mundane entries about work and school, it happened again.

March 20 1971

...Elvis called to ask if we could come to the house a little early before going to Howard Johnson's. Terry and I drove up the back driveway and parked. Charlie and Richard were already dressed and downstairs. Charlie told me to go to the next room if I wanted to find Elvis. Elvis was in the room and when he saw me he said, "Hi Baby, I've just been waiting for y'all to get here so we can have some fun." I walked over to him and he put both his arms around my waist and kissed my stomach. We sat on the floor by the TV and he talked to Charlie for awhile. I just sat there. Terry came in and sat down too. Charlie got some stuff together to take to Howard Johnson's while we all just sat around. Elvis went to get ready and Terry and I had fun just looking around without anyone else there. There were lots of pictures of Elvis and his family from a long time ago. Charlie said we could go ahead to the motel if we wanted and they would be

119

right behind us. We waited in the car for a few minutes until they got there and Elvis came over and opened both of the car doors for us. He said he loved the "Vomit Comet," and we both knew he was only kidding. We all grabbed stuff to carry and went into the room. People started getting there in just a few minutes. Elvis walked over to me and said, "I need to see my Pretty Lips soon without all these people being around. You're driving me crazy!" He kept rubbing his hands all over my back and shoulders and I felt like I was melting. It was fantastic. There were some new girls there that I think were friends of Priscilla's. They kept staring at me all night. I'm not worried about them telling her anymore. After about an hour I went next door with Terry to watch TV. We sat at the end of the bed and ate sandwiches. Charlie came over and asked us if we were OK, then said he'd fix us a drink if we wanted one. I got a coke to drink and he said I need more than a coke if I was going to have any fun. Everyone was getting tired of sitting in one room, and I guess they followed us to the next room just to see what was going on and to talk. People started telling stupid jokes and laughing. Elvis acted like they were funny. Elvis and I didn't do a lot tonight. Elvis just sat by me for a long time and watched TV. He kept saying, "I love to be with you," and I would just smile. He said I had sexy lips and I would always be called "Pretty Lips" by everyone and not just him. We stayed until about 3:00 and went home to bed...

With my heart beating just a little harder, and with feelings I had foolishly thought forgotten, I read the entry from two days later.

March 22 1971

...Elvis called and said we were going to the movies tonight and to get there about 11:00. Charlie was already there and Gene was there too. He thinks he's so cute but he isn't. Terry and I stayed up front with Charlie and talked for a long time. Elvis was inside and walked up front once he saw me and winked at me. We got a coke and some popcorn to eat and went to sit down. We sat two rows behind Elvis. He kept turning around and asking if we liked the show. I said yes. He got up after awhile and went up front. I waited a long time and he didn't come back so I got up and went up there. Everybody looked at me as if I was crazy! When Elvis saw me he asked what took me so long. I said I didn't know I was supposed to, but I wanted to see him so I did. He started kissing me all over my neck and lips, and he held me tight in his arms. Charlie and a few people were up there talking, but I didn't care. He said we better go back in and watch the movie for a little while, and he let me go. I went back into the movie and sat down with

Terry, and in a few minutes Elvis came back too. Terry said she was tired and didn't want to stay late so I told Elvis we had to go. Went home and went to bed...

After reading about Terry being tired that night, it made me recall just how tired I was after those late night meetings with Elvis. I was just about to finish my senior year in high school, and was working about 25 hours a week at Lowenstein's. Sleep seemed to be something I had very little of those days, and there was no way I wasn't going to see Elvis when he called. As it turns out, that call came a few days later.

March 24 1971

...Charlie called and said we were going to the movies tonight. We went to the house and drove up the back driveway. They weren't ready to leave when we got there, so we just waited outside. Charlie came out first and got in the car, and when Elvis came out he walked over to our car. I was leaning up against the side of the car and he asked me if I was ready for a wild, passionate night of fun. I just laughed and said I guess so. He took my hands and put them around his neck and said, "Well let's get started then!" He started kissing me so long and hard I could hardly get my breath. (He really started pressing against me hard and I didn't know if he was going to quit. I looked at him and said we had better wait until later.) I got in

the car and Terry and I followed them to the movie. We all parked around in the back. Terry and Charlie went inside and Elvis and I waited out back for awhile. He rubbed his hands all over me and it felt so good. I scratched my nails across his chest, and I could feel his skin under his shirt. He said he loved it, but I told him we had better go on in. Went and sat down with Terry, and then we went up front to get something to eat. We talked to Charlie for awhile and to the guy who was with him. In the movie, Elvis kept winking at me all night in front of everybody, and I got up halfway through the show and walked up front. Elvis got up in a few minutes and came up to be with me. We went to the couch in the men's room and made out for a long time. When we came out, Elvis had his arm around me and started talking to some guy I didn't know. While he was talking, he would just stop in the middle of saying something and start kissing my hair. I didn't kiss him back. I just stood there all the while he was rubbing his hand up my shirt and on my back and waist. I can't believe he did that. We went back and watched some more of the movie. He kept rubbing his hand all over the top of my legs and a little up my top and would lean across the seat and whisper in my ear. Terry said we had better go before it got too late and he said, "Kathy isn't going anywhere till I say so!" I just smiled and he would kiss me again. Finally after about another hour, Terry said she meant it, and that we would be in trouble if we were late. So Elvis kissed me hard and then walked me to the back door. He cupped my face in his hands and kissed me softly on my forehead and told us to be careful going home. He said he would call me soon. Went home and went to bed...

After that night the entries turned back to Gary, and it seemed like we were in a good period of our relationship. He seemed to be attentive to me at work and picked me up many days after school. We often went out to eat, and he took me to the drive-in movie a couple of times. He told me I was pretty and he finally asked me to his brother's wedding. Gary had a twin brother who was getting married in June. We hung around together all the time, so it wasn't like I didn't know him, or know about the wedding. I took it as a sign that Gary really didn't like me when he didn't invite me to go with him. Then one night, after he brought me home from a date, he asked me. I jumped at the invite, and that was when I thought Gary and I had a real future together.

But in my state of emotional confusion, in the back of my mind there was always Elvis, and it wasn't long before I went back to him.

April 2, 1971

...Gary called and said he would pick me up about 6:30 for our date. Waited for him until 8:00 and then he called and said he couldn't

make it. I was so mad! Sat around and watched TV. When I was about to go to bed, Elvis called and said they were going to the movies tonight and to please try to come. About 10:30 we left. We were there early but a lot of people were already there. Terry and I went in the theater but everyone was still talking and waiting for Elvis to get there. We walked around the lobby for awhile and then went in and got a seat. We sat right behind Elvis. When Elvis came in, and before Priscilla sat down, he leaned over the seat and kissed me before he sat down. I thought I would die! During the movie, he kept putting his arm behind Priscilla and rubbed his hand on my legs. We went up front about three times and made out but nothing great happened. Once when we were up front Elvis took off his belt and let me try it on. It was big and wide and it was beautiful, but it wouldn't fit me and kept sliding down to the floor. Elvis just laughed. I love it when he smiles and laughs at me. We talked to Charlie a lot tonight, and when Elvis would walk by, he would hum in my ear and act silly. We didn't stay too late, and went home about 2:30 and went to bed.

Sitting in the quiet of my kitchen, with the diary opened before me, I know how this story ends--or at least what it has led me to. But in what sometimes seems like only yesterday, when I was young and alone in my room filling these pages, I did not have that vision. What would I change if I could? I suppose that's something all of us ask at one time or another. For me, I'm not sure I would have done anything differently. But for me to step back in time and relive my past, I only have to turn a page…

11

꒦꒷꒦꒷꒦

FROM THE KITCHEN WINDOW, I CAN SEE the lightening of the nighttime sky, but there is much that still demands to be remembered. The diary lays open before me, and its power over me remains strong. I am powerless to stop until I have turned the last page and read the final line. I guess if I was honest with myself, it has been this way since I first found it hiding on the shelf. For me, it is like a time machine, with the ability to transport me to another age. In April of 1971, my age was 18, and I had no idea of the changes that lay before me.

I began to see Gary much more frequently, and my time spent with Elvis began to diminish. The main reason for that was because he was so busy, and he was in and out of town all the time. I almost never knew where he was or what he was doing. When he would come back to town, he would call, but many times mother wouldn't let me go. Between work and school and dates with Gary almost every night, mother had grown weary of me being gone all the time. I believe at this time in my life, my relationship with my mother was the most strained it had ever been.

For me, it came to a head about two weeks before I graduated. I had been seeing Gary regularly, and one night after work he asked me to the movies. Mother didn't want me go, but after we argued for awhile she relented. She told me I had to be home by 11:00. I remember how childlike it made me feel to have a curfew. In my mind I was practically grown. I guess like all kids my age, I felt like that status came with your high school diploma. As much as I hated doing it, I agreed to mother's terms and went to the show with Gary. I guess you know how that turned out.

The diary entry highlights the evening and the proverbial final straw when it came to my desire to leave the house. Mother was up and waiting for me when I came home 11 minutes late. I told her about the slow moving train in the industrial park, which had blocked the road and made us late. Mother wasn't listening or just didn't care, but she grounded me just the same. I just couldn't believe she was being so unreasonable over a measly 11 minutes.

I spent most of the next day crying in my room. Gary tried calling me several times, but mother wouldn't let me talk to him. Oh how I wanted to be out of that house, and for a long time that's all I thought about. I decided right then, if Gary ever asked me to marry him, I would do it. I suppose then I thought that was the only way I would be able to leave. All I know for sure, was at that time in life, I just wanted to be out of the house and away from mother.

It's funny now when I think about mother, and about how much our relationship has changed. I see her regularly and enjoy our time together very much. There is so much love between us; love I couldn't comprehend back then. Perhaps it can only be felt or understood with motherhood, for it is the same way I feel about my own children. Too bad life has to be that way, but I suspect as long as there are teenagers it shall be so.

I skim through the diary and read a few lines about my graduation. Gary came and gave me an opal ring for a gift. A few weeks after that, I quit working at Lowenstein's and got a job at the hospital as a blood tech. Gary took a job as manager at Lowenstein's, and we began to spend all of our time together. I started spending time meeting his family and had supper with them quite a lot. At one of the meals, his aunt welcomed me to the family, and at first I didn't know what she meant. Gary got all embarrassed and said he meant we might get married, then quickly added, "I never said we were getting married!"

After that night we talked occasionally about getting married someday, but it was never anything serious. In late October of that year, Gary told me he had something to tell me. He said if we were to have any future together, there was something in his past he needed to share with me. He told me he had been arrested once when he was 18, and I was a little shocked. In Gary's opinion, it wasn't that big of a deal, so I didn't let it become one with me. I suspect it was something daddy had known all along and was the primary reason he never seemed to like him. Still, I thought it was a sweet thing to share with me and made me feel like he trusted me completely.

After he shared his past with me, I felt like I had to do the same. I told him about my relationship with Elvis. I suppose I was just caught up in the moment, but it came out with a bang. For a moment, he had a surprised look on his face, and then he just laughed. Then he realized I wasn't trying to be funny when I started to cry. He wanted to know everything, and the words slipped from my mouth. Then he asked me if I had been with him since we had been dating. I couldn't make myself lie to him, so I told him the truth. He was in total shock, but it only lasted a few moments. He told me then if we were ever going to have a future together I had to choose right now between him or Elvis.

Can anyone imagine what was going through my head? On that night, I had to choose between someone I was beginning to have strong feelings for and someone I loved. It was an ultimatum no girl should have to face, but I could tell Gary's feelings had been hurt. I made a choice that night and told him I wouldn't see Elvis anymore. It was a promise I wasn't sure I could keep, but I had given him my word and I was certainly going to try.

Sometime in November of 1971, my promise to Gary was put to the ultimate test. Terry was home for the weekend, and we were just out in the driveway shooting baskets. A car pulled up and a man in a suit got out of the car. He introduced himself and said he was Elvis' attorney. Terry and I both thought we had seen him with Elvis at one time or another, but we couldn't remember for sure. He said everyone was going to the movie tonight, and then said, "Elvis really wants you to come!"

Terry just looked at me wondering what I was going to say. She knew I had made a promise not to see him anymore, and I guess she was curious to see if I would keep it. I said I didn't know he was back in town, and the man said he had returned last night. I really didn't know what to tell him about going to the movie, so I just said maybe. Then he told me that Elvis was very fond of me, and then said something I had heard many times from Elvis in the past. He said, "You know, Priscilla isn't always going to be around, and when she is gone, you will be able to write your own ticket. All you have to do is ask." I thanked him for the invite and then he got into his car and left.

Terry and I just stood there looking at each other. At first I didn't know what to say or what I should do. Then it became clear to me that I had to see him and would have to break the promise I made. I called Elvis on the phone and he said it was alright to come over if I wanted. Terry offered to go with me, but I felt like this was something I had to do on my own. I got in the car and drove straight to Graceland.

I had no problem getting the guard to let me in. I had known him for awhile and he was always friendly whenever Terry and I were there. I drove up the back drive and Richard let me in when I knocked on the door. He seemed surprised to see me, but went right away to get Elvis. In a minute he came back and said I could wait in the other room for Elvis to come down. I went into the room and started looking at all the pictures, just like Terry and I had done once before.

It felt strange to be in that room by myself, and I believe it was because I had never been here when it was light. It was always late at night when I had been with Elvis--either here at Graceland, or at the movies. Perhaps it was the room's brightness that finally opened my eyes. As I looked at the pictures scattered about the room, I came across a more recent one of Elvis and Priscilla, and a very young Lisa Marie sitting on Elvis' lap. I was taken by how much she looked like Elvis and about how happy they all seemed to look whenever the picture was taken. They were a family--the reality of it was as if I had been punched in the stomach.

I would have no future with Elvis, at least not the one I wanted. I didn't want his money or his possessions, or the fame that made all those things possible. I wanted him, and I knew that was the one thing he could never give me. Looking around the room at the pictures and the memorabilia hanging on the walls was enough to tell me that. He belonged to the world, and he always would. I would only be fooling myself to think otherwise. I looked at the photo of him with Priscilla and Lisa Marie again and told myself I didn't want that to be me. I knew if I stayed with him, it would only be a matter of time before someone else took my place. As much as I loved him, I knew the clock was nearing the midnight hour, and the fairy tale I had been living was coming to an end.

Elvis startled me when he came into the room, and it was if I was seeing him for the first time. It had been some time since I had last been with him, and there was much about him that seemed to have changed. His hair was quite a bit longer and his side burns were so bushy. He looked tired and slightly run down, but his eyes seemed as bright as ever.

Still there was a difference to them. I thought perhaps he was only tired, but in the back of my mind I knew it was more than that. Elvis the King was now so much larger than the man, and the toll it was taking on him was evident. I suppose in the end, his legend and persona were greater than a mortal man's body could contain. For him, I believe it was the beginning of the end. The price for being the brightest star in the sky is high, for eventually it is consumed by its own radiance, leaving only a dark hole in its place. He was the bright star in the night sky--as anyone who was lucky enough to meet him knows--and such a hole he left in our hearts when he departed this world.

He walked across the room and took me into

his arms. At first, I was powerless in his embrace, and I didn't resist when he kissed me hard on the lips. He told me how much he had missed me, and before I could stop him, he was melting me with soft kisses on my neck. A wave of desire crashed over me, and I was within seconds of surrendering myself to him. I loved him so much, but then I remembered the promise I had made to Gary. I summoned my strength, and for the first time in the two-and-a-half years we had been seeing each other, I pushed myself away from him. I said no, and he seemed surprised by my rebuff. He asked me what was wrong, and for a moment I didn't know what I was going to say or do. But then, like the brightness of the room, it became clear to me-- this had to end.

I told him everything I had been going through, and that I couldn't do it anymore. He understood, and we talked for awhile. I knew this was the thing I would miss the most--just being with him and talking. Although he was much older than me, sometimes when we talked he seemed to be much closer to my age. I loved him so much, but above everything else, he was my friend and always would be. I turned to leave the room and he called out to me, "I love you Kathy Tatum!" I didn't even turn around because I didn't want him to see me crying. He had always called me "Laughing Eyes," and that was the way I wanted him to remember me. I had no idea at the time that those were the last words he would ever say to me, or that it was the last time I would ever see him again.

I practically ran from the house and don't even remember if I told Richard goodbye. I got in the car and drove to the gate, all without realizing it was the last time I would ever be at Graceland. Not far from the gates, I stopped in a store parking lot and must have cried for 30 minutes or more. The thought crossed my mind a few times to go back to him, but I knew this was for the best. I gathered myself together and wiped my tears. I went back home knowing that while I had done what was for the best, it didn't make it any easier. I wondered why doing what was best had to hurt so bad. I guess sometimes I still do.

Over the course of time, I came to accept the fact I would never be with Elvis again--at least not in that way. My life returned to normal, and on Christmas day 1971, Gary proposed to me. He gave me a large stuffed dog with the ring tied on a string around its neck. Probably not the most romantic of proposals, but I accepted without hesitation.

The rest is history as they say, and in the predawn light of my kitchen, the diary calls me back...

12

❧❧❧❧❧

AFTER THE CHRISTMAS OF 1971, GARY AND I started making plans for a June wedding. Reading the entries leading up to the big day, I can see the road wasn't always smooth. There are many entries about Gary making me mad about something, but there are also just as many where he was sweet. I suppose I just wanted to be married so bad I just never saw the writing on the wall. I wanted a grown up version of my playhouse with real linoleum floors. Instead of my dolls, I wanted children, and like all girls, I wanted a husband like my daddy. To be perfectly honest, I was more in love with the idea of being in love than I actually ever was with Gary.

In early June of 1972, there is a small entry about our rehearsal dinner, but the one that probably sums it up the best came on…

June 9 1972

...Worked. Went to clean apartment and Gary finally came home late to help. I fussed at him a little. Went to get something to eat and then I took Gary home. He said goodnight Miss Tatum. I came home and washed hair and watched TV. Wedding day tomorrow so I went to bed...

That was the last entry in the diary. Why I had stopped after all that time I really don't know. Perhaps I no longer needed to put my feelings in writing and thought I now had someone to share them with. Maybe I thought that part of my life was over, and the diary no longer had a purpose. Whatever the reason, after almost 5 years of continuous entries, the pages fell silent. Now in the silence of my kitchen, my mind fills in the pieces of my life that were left unwritten.

After our wedding Gary and I moved into a small apartment near his parents. Soon after that, we bought a small house in the country. In July of 1973 our son Dax was born. Two years later in September 1975, our second son Cade was born. We moved to a larger house in town, and not long after that Gary lost his job at Lowenstein's. I remember worrying how we were going to make it. Then a woman I worked with at the time found out about our situation and said her husband was the chief of police. Gary submitted his application the next day, and her husband hired Gary as a dispatcher.

Things were a whole lot brighter after that, but it didn't last very long. One warm August afternoon in 1977, as I pushed Dax and Cade in the swing, the radio brought me to my knees. Like the rest of the world, a piece of my heart was ripped away when I heard that Elvis had died. I was shocked and cried uncontrollably. I couldn't believe he was gone; I called Terry right away to see if she had heard the news. We talked for awhile, but it just didn't seem real; we both hung up wishing we had gone to see him one last time. It was always something we had talked about doing, but as is usually the case, the time never seemed right.

After I talked with Terry, I wondered if there was something I could have done to have kept this from happening. I knew from the newspapers a few months after Gary and I were married that he had filed for divorce. He had always asked me to be patient, and I had told him I would. I wondered if things might have been different if I had. For awhile, I blamed myself and felt like I had let him down.

Then I remembered the last time I had seen him, and the way it had ended for us. I could tell that I had hurt him, but there was an understanding between us. He understood my dreams for the future, and he laughed when I told him about my playhouse from my childhood. He had offered to buy me the biggest one they made, but then he smiled because he knew that wasn't what I meant. We talked as friends that day, and it is perhaps the thing I miss the most. I suppose I knew him as few others had, without all the showmanship and glitter. I saw him when he was at his best, when he was just being himself, and that is the way I shall always remember him.

What was it about me that attracted him in the first place? As I have said before, there were many girls at the gate the day we first met. I guess that's something I will never know. What I do know was that I never asked him for anything, and I believe that was something that he rarely encountered. All I have from him are the love beads he freely placed around my neck and the heart-filled memories of our times together. These are the days of his life which are etched into my mind and are scribed in the pages of my diary. It is where they belong, and where they shall ever remain, until the day when we shall meet again.

What killed him? There have been many books and stories about his demise. Most are pure speculation and I can only tell you what I know for a fact. In the over two years we were together, I never saw him put any poison into his body. Period! The absolute strongest thing I ever saw him with was the bourbon and coke we sometimes shared together.

Was it around? I suppose it was, but that is something I have no direct knowledge of. In the end, each of us is responsible for our own actions, but I believe it was those closest to him who are most to blame. There is no need to name them, for all who are familiar with his entourage know who they were. They were the users of his wealth and fame, and the corruptors of his mind. They were the basket of rotten fruit, which eventually caused the sweetest of apples to rot. Some of them are no longer with us, and the ones that are I have no use for. It is no different today than it was all those years ago, and that is the way I choose to leave it.

For me, life went on and a little over a year after Elvis' death my daughter Brittney was born. Two years after her, Tatum came into our lives. About that time Gary started working for a major shipping company in Memphis. He stayed on the road all the time, and when he was home he never really was. I had to look no further than the pages of my diary to see what had always been important to Gary. His friends and whatever he wanted to do always seemed to come first. It was no different when we were dating, and I was only fooling myself to think it would be any different after we were married. It's all there in the diary, so I guess I have no one to blame but myself.

With Gary gone most of the time, and four kids under the age of eight, I had to take work with flexible hours. I started cleaning a couple of stores three or four days a week. I would bring all the kids with me and feed them breakfast before the older ones went to school. Then with the younger ones in tow, I scrubbed and cleaned the floors. I suppose cleaning just came natural to me, and I still remember how Daddy had laughed at me when I swept the dirt on the barn floor. The kids call it O.C.D., but to me there was only one way to clean--the right way.

Over time I started adding more businesses, and before long I was also cleaning private homes. I liked the flexibility these jobs gave me; it gave me the time I needed to take care of my kids. But there was something missing in my life, and after 20 years of marriage I needed to find it. Gary and I had grown apart, and I believe that was how he wanted it. I asked him for a divorce and he didn't object. I don't think he ever really understood why. It takes more than just kids and a husband to make a marriage, and like a wood stove that is left unattended, the fire eventually goes out. The metal grate grows cold to the touch, and after awhile it doesn't make much sense to huddle around it for warmth. We parted amicably, so at least we had that.

After our divorce, I got by as I always had by cleaning homes and businesses. I also babysat for some of my neighbors for extra income. About a year after our divorce, I was introduced to Phil by a mutual friend. We dated for awhile and then decided to get married. About a year later, our son Forrest was born. We live on the land Phil's family has owned for generations, and it is where Forrest grew up. Now 20 years later, his plans are to leave and perhaps become an EMT with the fire department. I wish him only the best as I have for all of my children.

The rays from the morning sunrise fall on my eyes and snap me back to the present. I have spent the entire evening immersed in my diary and my memories, and the time for them is over. I carefully close the diary and put it on the counter. Phil and Forrest will soon be up, and I must get their breakfast started. Phil likes to get an early start on the day, doing repairs to mowers and engines for people in town. Phil is a handyman like my daddy used to be, and Forrest works alongside of him trying to learn all he can. I continue to clean homes and businesses four days a week and will soon have to get started on my way.

With breakfast over and the men out the door, I busy myself with the breakfast dishes. The morning paper is on the table, and the headline is about the candlelight vigil at Graceland tonight. A huge crowd is expected, as it is almost every year, and I can't believe it has been 37 years. I cannot bring myself to read the article, so I get my diary off the counter and take it back to the closet. I look at the picture of Elvis and me one more time and wonder where all the years have gone. I carefully put everything back into the ziplock bag and return it to the back of the top shelf. I tell myself this is where it belongs, and I hope to quell the flood of emotions I now feel. I suspect it will not be that easy.

I know that what I have stirred up will not easily settle, and I suppose that's how it will always be. Regrets? I guess I have a few, but it's mostly things I would never change. I cannot regret marrying Gary, for that would mean giving up my precious children. I cannot get back my high school years, and I'm not sure I would want to even if I could. There are times that I wished I could have shared my secret about Elvis in school, but to have done so would have ended it much too soon.

Dating was something else I may have missed out on, because what pimple-faced high school boy could compete with Elvis? No dance or formal could ever compare to an evening of being held in his arms, or feeling his kisses upon my neck. I guess when I think about it now, there's probably very little about my life that I would change. I am content with my life, and my place in it, and I guess that's all anyone can ask for.

I sat down on the bed and slid my top dresser drawer open. Under some of my things is the velvet-lined box which contains my most prized possessions. I took it out and carefully opened the lid. Inside is my first grownup Christmas present from daddy--the watch with diamond chips on the side and a brown leather band. Next to the watch are the love beads that Elvis gave to me, and I take them out and hold them in my hand. I press them to my face; it's almost as if I can still smell the cologne he was wearing that night. It is probably only my imagination, but still there are tears in my eyes. I put them back into the box, and as I wipe my eyes, I realize how tired I am. I think I shall have no problem sleeping tonight.

I lay my head down on the pillow and hope that if I am lucky tonight, I shall…

…Dream…

It is dark and I am on my way to Graceland. I drive the "Vomit Comet" past the mourners with their tears and their candles and wind my way up the drive to the back door. Elvis is already outside waiting for me and he climbs into the front seat beside me. He looks exactly the same as the last time I saw him. He smiles at me as we drive past the mourners and travel far out into the country.

We stop on the top of a hill, surrounded by beautiful wild flowers for as far as the eye can see. There, illuminated by the moon, stands my playhouse. Inside are the pasteboard stove and refrigerator, and the real linoleum floors I loved as a child. I invite Elvis in and we sit at the table and talk about everything and nothing, much as we used to. We talk the night away, and as the sun begins to rise, I tell him I must go.

When he gets up from the table, I tell him he is free to stay here. This was my sanctuary when I was a child, and now it is yours for as long as you like. It is my gift to you, and you are welcome here anytime you want. Here you will be safe, and no one can bother you in the house my daddy has built. With a final kiss the dream ends...

That is the dream I would share with him, if such a thing were possible. Who is to say what is or isn't? For sometimes things which seem beyond the realm of possibility have a way of coming true.

I was never a beautiful princess--at least I never thought so. I didn't live in a magical kingdom with a whimsical name, but rather in a mid-south city named Memphis. There was no shining castle atop a mountain bathed in a golden glow, but there was a storied mansion of white, known simply as Graceland. Contained within the pages of this true life fairy tale, there is no mention of a handsome prince. Instead, there was an extraordinary King…

The End

About the Authors

Kathy resides in rural West Tennessee with her husband Phil and their son Forrest. When she isn't rescuing stray animals, she keeps a busy schedule cleaning houses and businesses in the area. Always on the go (something she got from her Daddy), she loves spending her free time with her five children and five grandchildren.

Mark resides in the suburbs of Memphis with his wife Laurie; a Family Practice Physician. Married thirty-five years, they have two children, Lindsey and Ryan. Mark loves to hunt and fish and enjoys his quiet time while riding his Harley. A stay-at-home dad for the past twenty-six years, Mark is the consummate "domestic engineer". With the children grown and on their own, he is now free to pursue a new career in writing.

.